# And Then There Were Two

## Children and Second Language Learning

TERRY PIPER

Pippin Publishing Limited

Edited by Dyanne Rivers
Designed by John Zehethofer
Printed and bound by Kromar Printing Ltd.

**Canadian Cataloguing in Publication Data**

Piper, Terry
    And then there were two : children and second
language learning

(The Pippin teacher's library ; 15)
Includes bibliographical references.
ISBN 0-88751-060-4

1. English language — Study and teaching as a
second language (Elementary).* 2. English language — Study and teaching as a second language (Secondary).* I. Title. II. Series.

PE1128.A2P56 1993          372.65'21          C93-093934-4

ISBN 0-88751-060-4

10   9   8   7   6   5   4   3   2   1

# CONTENTS

For Grace and Earnest Ridpath, who were my first and best teachers.

. . . . . . . . . . . . . . .

# PREFACE

The idea for this book came to me as I was flying across the Pacific to Beijing. I'd just finished reading Mary Ashworth's *The First Step on the Longer Path: Becoming an ESL Teacher* and was thinking about how remarkably well the book fulfilled the promise of its title. Having learned during the years I worked with Mary in ESL teacher education that the path is fairly long and rocky, the question that naturally occurred to me was, What's the *next* step?

Thinking back on my years with Mary and those since, when I've been "on my own," I concluded that the next step is to focus on the learner. Surely teachers are curious and need to know more about how children learn second languages. And so, rather brazenly, I set a goal—to sketch in these pages what resembles a mural more than a detailed portrait of ESL learners. Under what conditions do they become bilingual? How are they alike and how do they differ in what they bring to the task? What strategies do they adopt as they go about learning a second language? What role does their native language play in the process? What happens if they have other special needs? And, finally, how can this information guide us in planning ESL curricula and programs?

In the following chapters, I've tried to provide initial answers to these questions. I must stress, however, that the journey doesn't end on the last page of this book. This book simply represents one more step along Mary's path. I hope it's one that carries you closer to your goal of becoming an ESL teacher or, if you already teach ESL, answers some of the questions that may have occurred to you.

# CHILDREN'S SECOND

# LANGUAGE LEARNING

$M$ost English speakers are surprised to learn that people who speak only one language form a minority of the world's population and that most people function in two or more languages. While few people are truly "balanced" bilinguals or polyglots who feel equally comfortable with all their languages, the fact is that most of the world's population functions in more than one language. Given this, it's somewhat surprising that so much attention is paid in the English-speaking world to the matter of learning an additional language. If so many people seem to do it so easily, then just what is the problem?

The simplest answer is that there really isn't one. Given ample opportunity and time, most people can learn as many languages as they want or need to. But as teachers charged with the responsibility of adding English to the linguistic inventory of non-English-speaking children, we must be concerned with precisely these matters—providing ample and effective opportunity and using time as effectively as possible.

This chapter will look briefly at how children become bilingual. First, we'll examine the conditions that lead to bilingualism in preschoolers, then we'll turn our attention to language learning in the classroom. In focusing on the differences between language acquisition at home and at school, we'll see that there's the potential for conflict between children's informal language learning in the home and the more formal experience of the school.

As teachers, we might well ask why it's necessary to study second language learning in preschoolers when school-aged children are our major concern. Obviously, we're primarily interested in how school-aged children learn English as an additional language. But it's equally important for us to know something about the experience of younger children. The reason is simple—the better we understand children's previous successful experiences of learning, the better we can plan an effective language-learning environment for children in school. We'll begin, then, by talking about home bilingualism before turning our attention to school bilingualism and, finally, the potential for conflict between the home and school experience.

## Home Bilingualism

The term "home bilingualism" refers to the language-learning achievement of children who learn two languages from birth. It also refers to any other second language learning that begins before children start school, whether that learning actually takes place at home, in daycare or preschool, or any other place they come into contact with a second language. Researchers have long been interested in this early bilingualism and have used a variety of methods to investigate both the learning process and the effects of early bilingualism. The following summarizes the most consistent and interesting of their findings:

*In general, young children acquire two or more languages in much the same way as they learn different registers—socially defined varieties—of the same language.*

Children occasionally mix languages, particularly the vocabularies when they may, for example, temporarily assign objects a single name. For the most part, however, they keep the languages distinct and experience little confusion.

I've often told the story of a conversation I had with a five-year-old Portuguese child named Lanny. The story, which I first recounted in an article published in *Language Arts*, happened when I was conducting a research project in northern British Columbia several years ago. One morning in November, I was sitting with Lanny at a table in the back of the kindergarten classroom trying to persuade her to identify some pictures and thus provide me with the data I needed for my study. Lanny, however, was more interested in talking about her own life and so the conversation turned to her newborn baby brother. She was impressed by how tiny and helpless he was, and observed that he couldn't walk or feed himself or talk. I ventured to suggest that the cries and other noises he made were his way of talking now and that, as he grew older, he would learn to speak just as she did.

"What language do you think he'll speak?" I asked.

I might as well have asked how many home runs Babe Ruth hit in his best year. The look on her face telegraphed her opinion of the question. I tried again.

"How many languages do you speak, Lanny?"

Overwhelmed by the inanity of this question, she turned her attention to the pictures. I decided to try one more time.

"How many languages do you speak?"

Summoning all her patience, this time she answered firmly, "One."

Not knowing when to keep quiet, I persisted, "Which one?"

Without hesitating, she answered in a tone that made it clear that she'd had quite enough of this nonsense, "Mine."

I've told this story so often because I think it reveals a great deal about how Lanny viewed her two languages. Apparently, for her, English and Portuguese constituted a single language with two registers, one that she used at home and the other that she used at school. Lanny appeared to have learned, as most children do, that one variety of language is used at home and another at school.

*Children seem to recognize differences in the sound systems of their languages, seldom mixing their pronunciations.*

Even when children adopt a word from language A for use in language B, they give it a pronunciation consistent with language B. For example, in a school lunchroom last year, I heard a six-year-old Chinese child identify "bao and butter," using the Chinese word for bread but without the tonal qualities it would have had in Chinese. She had learned the English word "butter" presumably because most Chinese people do not eat butter and she had no Chinese word for it.

*Bilingualism does no harm. Children are capable of learning two languages simultaneously without damaging either.*

In other words, proficiency in one language is not achieved at the expense of the other. By the time bilingual children reach school age, almost all will have reached the same level of linguistic proficiency in both languages as their monolingual peers in either. But they will, of course, have the advantage of knowing an additional language.

A cautionary note should be sounded here, however. As we look for examples of children who begin school with proficiency in more than one language, we find that a great many come from immigrant families. Many of these children function well in both languages, having learned English either from their parents or peers. The English proficiency of others, however, may be limited because they've learned English from parents who were not themselves fluent. When these children come to school speaking English, their vocabulary or ways of expressing themselves may be limited. In some cases, they may have pronunciation problems because their parents' accented English was their primary model. These children are, nevertheless, considered bilingual—they can, after all, function in two languages. But if their English is greatly limited, they will need to learn what is essentially a *third* language— standard English or the English of the school.

*Children can learn languages under a variety of "normal" conditions.*

I recently met a six-year-old Vietnamese child named Quy who spoke very good English even though his parents were still at the beginning level in their English courses. I discovered that he had learned English at the daycare center he attended from the time he was three until he was five. This is only one normal condition for language acquisition. Some children learn one language from their mother and another from their father. Others have parents who speak the same language but have a grandparent or babysitter who speaks another. Or everyone in the home may speak the same language while the child's playmates speak another.

Still another normal condition is for both parents to be bilingual, switching back and forth between languages. Children in this situation, however, run a small risk of mixing the languages. It seems that confusion between languages is minimized when the two are kept distinct. Children seem to have little trouble learning the separate languages of their two parents, or the language of their parents and the language of their peers or other caretaker. Sometimes, however, children use different criteria for deciding which language to use. In a study reported in 1967, for example, V. Ruke-Dravina found that children used their parents' language, Swedish, when playing with Latvian playmates inside theit own homes. Outside, however, they spoke Latvian with the same playmates.

*The age at which preschoolers encounter the second language doesn't seem to matter greatly.*

Whether preschoolers are exposed to two languages at birth or age two, three or four doesn't seem to affect the degree of proficiency they eventually attain. As long as the exposure continues, children are likely to become functioning bilinguals. Quy, the child mentioned earlier, began speaking English at age three; his brother attended the same daycare center beginning when he was two. Both children were equally proficient. The age at which children encounter a second language seems to be irrelevant, however, only with respect to home bilingualism. As we shall see later, the age at which learning a second language begins may become more critical once children reach school age.

*Children do not need to be "taught" a second language at home; they learn it much as they learn the first language.*

Because of this, certain observations about how children acquire a first language become important to our understanding of home bilingualism. For many children, it is inaccurate to refer to this early learning as second language acquisition, because what they're really doing is acquiring two first languages simultaneously. This is what happens when, for example, a child hears only English from an English-speaking mother and French from a French-speaking father. No doubt, there are a great many children like this in the English-speaking world, but what may be even more common are children whose parents speak the same language but who learn another language from babysitters, grandparents or other relatives. Because of their age and the circumstances under which they acquire the languages, these children are likely learning all their languages in much the same way monolingual children learn their single language.

Certain facts about first language acquisition are extremely important, then, to our understanding of home bilingualism. The most significant, of course, is that children don't learn language for its own sake but in tandem with and as a means of making sense of the world. Given this, there are several basic truths about first language acquisition that are also relevant to our understanding of second language learners:

*Children's learning progresses according to their degree of readiness.*

Parents don't insert language-learning time into their children's schedules—and it would do no good if they did. Neither would it help for a mother to coax and coach her three-month-old child to say "Mama" or "Dada" nor her two-year-old to recite the Gettysburg Address. Nature determines much of the timetable; the child determines the rest.

*Young children are, for the most part, in charge of their own learning.*

They may not *know* they're in charge, but they do determine what they learn and when. While they're constrained, of course, by their cognitive and physical maturity, their natural and robust curiosity about the world around them in large part inspires their early attempts at using language. Children's desire to explore the outside world provides the motivation that eventually leads them to develop the ability to ask to go outside to play. Similarly, children who want to find out for themselves the meaning of the words in a book or magazine start to ask parents or other readers to identify words for them and, in doing so, eventually learn to read.

*Play is important in children's learning.*

A great variety of language learning occurs as children play. Parents who rhyme and otherwise "play" with language witness the delight it brings infants. Imagine the language opportunities that even very young children have in their pretend roles as mommies, daddies or superheroes. Not only must they adopt the topics, language and registers of the roles they assume, but they must also begin to use language that isn't limited by real time and real events. Through play, they begin the process of decontextualizing language; that is, using language that doesn't refer to real people or objects in the present.

*Parents assume the role of facilitator, not instructor.*

Although parents are children's first and most enduring teachers, it would be a great mistake to think of them as instructors. We might like to think that we taught our children to talk, but the hard truth is that parents' true role in language learning is that of partners in daily interactions. The dialogues that take place between parents and children as they talk their way through activities as routine as washing hands or putting on pajamas or as special as decorating a birthday cake or putting up the Christmas tree provide the means for children to learn. Parents are collaborators in the making of conversation. They aren't always equal collaborators, of course, because when there is misunderstanding or miscommunication, it falls upon the parents, the more experienced users of the language, to make the necessary adjustments to facilitate collaboration.

*Learning is embedded in the socialization process.*

It's a good thing that children's days at home aren't divided into time periods the way they are at school. Imagine the miserable childhoods we would have endured if our parents had assigned us an hour to work on motor development, half an hour for memory development, twenty minutes for hygiene and an hour and a half for socialization into the family and community. Rather, children's learning at home occurs as an unfragmented whole. Children's early language learning is directed toward achieving full membership in the local society of the family and community.

Although they must reach certain biological stages before they can speak, children don't learn to say words because their biological clocks tell them it's time to do so but because language is the means through which people connect with one another. The language children develop to achieve group membership is social language and differs from the language of the school, as we shall see.

## School Bilingualism

School bilingualism refers to second language learning that begins at any time during the school years. However, it isn't the location of the school or the fact that children have reached five or six years of age instead of two, three or four that distinguishes home from school bilingualism; rather, as a number of researchers have observed, it's the quality and the type of language used in schools that is fundamentally different from the language of the home.

In *Children's Minds*, Margaret Donaldson noted that this difference is both linguistic and cognitive. She pointed out that before they begin school, children are quite capable thinkers, with their thought "directed outwards onto the real, meaningful, shifting, distracting world." Once they start school, however, they must learn "to turn language and thought in upon themselves," to direct their own cognitive processes in a thoughtful manner. In other words, children move from the concrete, meaning-centered language of the home to the abstract, inward-focused and largely decontextualized language of the school. As one child put it, teachers seem to talk about things that aren't there! In short, in the schooling process, children must learn to manipulate symbols and, if they are second language learners, they must learn these new thinking and language skills in an unfamiliar language.

Another way of distinguishing between home and school language is in terms of its function. Children acquire language as a way of participating fully in the social world around them. They acquire it as a means to an end—various ends, actually—and it's in considering the purposes to which young children put language that we understand the functions language serves.

The earliest functions of children's language are to get things done, interact with others, make believe or pretend, and receive and transmit information. These are largely learned in the home when children are very young. Later, they begin to use language to interpret, rather than simply report, their experiences, make logical connections, and express wishes, attitudes and judgments. These more abstract functions continue to develop through the school years.

Children's experiences with language at home and at school are also fundamentally different. I reported one of the worst examples of pointless school talk I've come across in my book, *Language for All Our Children*. It was transcribed from a conversation, if you can call it that, recorded in a kindergarten class by a research assistant. A five-year-old named Molly and her teacher were discussing a book:

*Teacher*: (Pointing to a dog illustrated in a picture book.) Molly, do you know what this is?
*Molly*: Yes.
*Teacher*: What is it?
*Molly*: A dog.
*Teacher*: Very good. And what's he playing with?
*Molly*: A ball.
*Teacher*: And what color is the ball?
*Molly*: Red.
*Teacher*: Right. (Pointing to a girl in the picture.) What is she wearing?
*Molly*: A skirt and blouse.
*Teacher*: What else?
*Molly*: Shoes and socks.
*Teacher*: That's good Molly. What do you think about this picture?
*Molly*: It's nice.

Molly's intelligence was normal and she was a native speaker of English. The teacher led the reluctant girl through an exercise in talk that had neither purpose nor value. Needless to say, this is an extreme example, but other less extreme examples also illustrate just how hollow school language can be. If Molly learned anything at all from this exchange, it was that there is little subject matter in teachers' talk and that teachers avoid talking about real things. She probably also learned that teachers ask questions to which they already know the answers and, if she is a typical child, that the only talk valued by the school is talk the school controls.

If this position seems extreme, just think about the number of times you've seen No Talking signs posted prominently in classrooms. It's telling that when children get into trouble at school, it's often for talking. Most parents of school-aged children will find the following dialogue at least somewhat familiar:

*Parent*: What did you do at school today?
*Child*: Nothing.
*Parent*: Nothing? Surely you did something!
*Child*: Nope.
*Parent*: Did you get into trouble?
*Child*: Just the usual.
*Parent*: You'll have to help me with this one. What's "the usual"?
*Child*: You know. Talking.
*Parent*: Oh, right. You were talking when you weren't supposed to.
*Child*: I'm *never* supposed to.

Who does most of the talking in classrooms? Actually, research provides a pretty clear answer to this question. In a recent study of talk in a grade three and a grade six classroom, Claire Staab found that either the class was quiet or the teacher was talking 78 per cent of the time. Think about what this means. If there are twenty-five children in the class, they must compete for a chance to talk during the remaining 22 per cent of class time, giving each of them less than 1 per cent of total "air time," or less than three minutes to talk during a five-hour school day.

Two additional facts in this study were also revealing. The first was that nearly 99 per cent of the teachers questioned claimed to believe that oral language is essential to learning in the content areas. The second was that the results were essentially the same as those reported in studies done twenty years ago—despite all the research and writing on the importance of children's talk that's been done in the interim.

What do teachers talk about? Because we do most of the talking, it's especially important to know what we're talking about. Once again, Claire Staab supplied some of the answers. She found that teachers spent nearly half (49 per cent) the total class activity time lecturing, suggesting that most of the talk children hear serves the function of informing. For an additional 29 per cent of the time, either the class was quiet or the teacher was giving directions to the students to work quietly on their own. This would suggest that language used to direct or control is the other mainstay of classroom talk.

We can clearly see that there is great potential for disharmony between children's experiences of language at home and at school. At home, parents encourage and respond to children's attempts to make meaning, reacting positively to all indications of progress. At school, teachers tend to demand accuracy and see errors as failures rather than partial successes. Teachers don't tend to share the responsibility for achieving effective communication as fully as parents. Children shoulder most of the burden and those who don't succeed may be characterized as lazy or slow.

In claiming that the language of the home differs fundamentally from the language of school and that, in general, it's the school that's deficient, I've relied heavily on arguments and research from first language literature. The problem exists equally for second language learners, a fact that hasn't escaped the notice of researchers in recent years. Jim Cummins, a prominent Canadian researcher, has not only recognized the difference between the language of the home and the language of school but has hypothesized that the two are connected in particular ways. In characterizing the difference between home and school bilingualism, he has claimed that children's success with language learning in school depends to a large degree on their language learning experience at home. He calls the language children acquire at home basic interpersonal communication skills and the language children must master to be successful at school cognitive academic language.

The research he and his colleagues conducted strongly indicates that successfully developing cognitive academic language proficiency depends largely on whether children have achieved a high degree of basic interpersonal communication skills. Furthermore, success in school seems also to depend on whether children have acquired at least some academic language proficiency before starting school. The kind of academic language proficiency children acquire in the home results from what are commonly called the literacy-based functions of language. In other words, children who have had stories read to them, who've seen their parents read for their own purposes, and who are generally surrounded by print have some knowledge of the academic purposes of language before they reach school.

We know that this relationship between home and school language applies to monolingual children. Time and again, researchers have shown that children who know about books before they get to school are more likely to succeed in the book-oriented world of the classroom. But let's think about second language learners, children who arrive at school with a language different from that of the school. They will have well-developed interpersonal communication skills in their first language and they may have some academic language proficiency as well, but they will have neither in the new language. They must begin again and, if Jim Cummins and his associates are right, they must begin in an environment dominated by cognitive academic language without first acquiring the basic interpersonal language on which to build.

Again, assuming that Jim Cummins' interdependence hypothesis is correct, these young children are educationally at risk, probably even more so than older children. The reason is that older children, who have had some formal education in their native language, will have developed greater cognitive academic proficiency in that language in addition to their basic interpersonal communication skills. Apparently, they're able to transfer their knowledge of the academic functions of language from their native language to the new language, giving them an advantage over younger learners who have less academic language proficiency to transfer.

This explanation is borne out by research conducted in the United States. In 1987, Virginia Collier reported the results of a study in which she analyzed the length of time required for English as a second language students to become proficient in school English. Looking at age of arrival among other variables, she found that the children who required more time to reach target proficiency levels were either under eight or over twelve.

For the younger learners, the reason seems to be that they have had little or no schooling and, therefore, have less experience of school language to transfer to the new language. While the older learners have had many years of schooling and thus more academic language proficiency to transfer, she attributes their difficulty to the increased demands placed on them by other subjects in the curriculum. Because the high school curriculum is more demanding than that of the elementary school and the language of instruction is far more abstract, students of this age falter.

We might well assume, then, that ESL children who begin schooling in English between the ages of eight and twelve experience the least difficulty. In an ideal educational world, these findings might indicate two logical courses of action. The first would be to educate children in their first language through the early primary years, from kindergarten through grade two or three, then transfer them to English. The second would be to provide special intensive academic English for children over twelve to prepare them to move as quickly as possible into age-appropriate subject-area classes.

Of course, the first option is not available. It is true that in some English-speaking countries, an attempt is made to offer limited educational programs to aboriginal people who speak different languages. But there are only a small number of these in relation to the non-English-speaking population. Few education systems have the resources to establish the primary education programs required to meet the needs of all aboriginal and immigrant non-English speakers. For example, in Halifax, Nova Scotia, where the immigrant population is small, it would be necessary to establish elementary school programs for children in as many as twenty different language groups, even though many of these programs might have only one child enrolled. The cost of doing this would be prohibitive, even if qualified teachers could be found.

The second course of action is more plausible and many school systems with large numbers of ESL students do attempt to provide intensive reception classes for them. But let's look at what happens all too often in practice. If children arrived during the early summer in time to spend two or three months studying English before the school year begins in September, then some of them might be ready to handle certain subjects immediately. However, in such a short time, few beginners are likely to learn enough English to write the papers required in high school English, history or geography classes, for example. In addition, few children are so cooperative about their arrival times, appearing instead in October or December or March. In these situations, it might seem desirable to delay their admission to regular classes until they've gained sufficient English proficiency to function.

This is simply not realistic for a number of reasons, however. In the first place, it has taken native English-speaking children twelve to fifteen years to reach their current level of language proficiency. Moreover, research has shown that it takes between three and seven years for non-English-speaking children to become proficiently bilingual. It is thus unrealistic to expect adolescent learners, even though they are at the height of their language-learning powers, to be proficient in English before they enter classes with native English-speaking peers.

In the second place, the students or their parents may object to having their schooling, which may have been interrupted already, delayed any further. Or they may resent the implication that they aren't ready to enter our educational system, which they may view as less demanding than the one they just left. For a number of reasons, then, these young people do not have the luxury of time and alternative solutions must be found.

# LEARNING STYLES

# AND STRATEGIES

In the previous chapter, I observed that children succeed in learning one, two or more languages under a wide variety of circumstances. Indeed, because bilingualism is the rule rather than the exception in most of the world, it would seem that learning a second language can't be too difficult. Yet we all know that learning an additional language is tough for some people who are simply less successful language learners than others. As teachers, we have a particular interest in understanding why this is true, especially if we hope to create learner-centered classrooms. We have a responsibility to focus our attention on how learners learn and what makes some more successful than others.

But how can we find out why some learners succeed when others fail? Experience and intuition tell us that learners differ in what they bring to the task of learning; that is, they bring different abilities to bear on intellectual activities. Learners also seem to go about the business of learning in vastly different ways. For the past ten years or so, teacher-researchers have begun to focus on the differences that exist *within* learners as well as those that exist *between* learners. These differences relate to learning styles and learning strategies.

## Learning Styles

Learning styles refer to the attributes that exist within learners, affecting the way they function intellectually. Learners' styles influence *all* their learning, not just language learning.

For example, some people are more field independent or tolerant of ambiguity than others, factors that influence *how* they approach the business of learning. Writers differ on precisely which inherent characteristics count as learning styles, but most agree on the importance of field dependence and independence, tolerance of ambiguity, and reflectivity and impulsiveness. In his chapter on cognitive variations in *Principles of Language Learning and Teaching*, H. Douglas Brown also includes left- and right-brain functioning within the general category of learning style.

FIELD DEPENDENCE AND INDEPENDENCE

We've all heard it said of certain people that they can't see the forest for the trees or, conversely, can't see the trees for the forest. Fortunately, perhaps, neither ability is called for in language learning. The reference is nonetheless apt because it describes a trait that is relevant to most human learning. Let's consider a more relevant example. Some people can read only in quiet surroundings while others can sit engrossed in a book in the middle of a crowded and very noisy airport, apparently oblivious to the bustle around them. The trait that distinguishes these two kinds of people—those who can't pick out an individual tree in the forest nor read in bedlam as opposed to those who can find the tree in the forest and take little notice of chaos—is their degree of field dependence or independence.

Field dependence is the tendency to see the big picture, to be more aware of the whole than of its parts. Field independence, in contrast, is the tendency to perceive a particular unit or item within a whole, independent of the other items or units it comprises. In learning, there are advantages to both field independence and dependence. Being field independent means that an individual is able to concentrate on particular tasks without being distracted by other, peripheral tasks. Field independent people tend also to be very analytical, able to take problems apart and deal individually with their component parts. Excessive field independence, however, makes it difficult to see anything beyond the immediate problem or situation.

Although one of the two traits eventually dominates in most people, some degree of the opposite trait tends to remain and is, in fact, desirable. For example, some field dependence is required in primarily field independent people so they can see the trees *and* the forest and read in the busy airport without missing the announcement of their flight. Conversely, field dependent people, so good at seeing the big picture, need some field independence so they can focus on particular tasks. It's detrimental to learning to be either excessively field independent or dependent.

In Western cultures, young children tend to be primarily field dependent, becoming more field independent as they mature. This is not to say that field independence is the desired state. In fact, for approximately half the population, this development continues until they become predominantly field independent, while the other half remains predominantly field dependent.

There is also a tendency in Western cultures for males to be field independent and females to be field dependent, though this is only a tendency and not a sex-linked trait. Douglas Brown found that people who are field independent also tend to be more independent, competitive and self-confident, while those who are field dependent are generally "more socialized," deriving much of their sense of self from other people. He said there is also a tendency for field dependent people to be more sensitive to the thoughts and feelings of others.

LEFT- AND RIGHT-BRAIN FUNCTIONING

The correlation between field dependence and independence and these other personality traits may exist because of another, more fundamental trait. In particular, it may be that people who are field independent are also independent, competitive, self-confident and analytical because, in processing information about the world, they make greater use of the left hemisphere of the brain than the right. Indeed, the distinction between left- and right-brain functioning may, in fact, underlie other traits associated with learning style.

When we talk about the left and right hemispheres of the brain, there is a tendency to think in polar terms. This is to say that it's easy to forget that the two hemispheres act in concert and, through the corpus callosum, the tissue that connects the two hemispheres, stay in regular communication. No one is wholly left- or right-brained unless, of course, there has been extensive damage to one hemisphere. Nevertheless, it seems that most people exhibit behavior that is consistent with dominance of one hemisphere or the other. For instance, people who are left-brain dominant tend to respond intellectually rather than intuitively in most situations. They control their feelings, remember names, are good at planning and organization, and rely on language for thinking and remembering. In class, they tend to prefer talking and writing, be analytical in their reading, favor logical problem-solving and prefer multiple-choice tests.

People who are right-brain dominant are generally more intuitive. They are more likely to show their emotions, remember faces better than names, be less organized and more spontaneous, and rely more on images for thinking and remembering. In class, they prefer drawing and manipulating objects, rely on synthesis rather than analysis in their reading, tend to solve problems intuitively rather than logically, and favor open-ended questions on tests.

Left- and right-brain functioning has been the subject of much scholarly research and popular speculation during the past two decades. While a great many scholars are still skeptical of the significance attached to the fact that some people show some hemispheric dominance, most concede that such dominance does exist and has some effect on people's intellectual lives.

It isn't at all clear how the distinction between field dependence and independence or left- and right-brain functioning influences second language learning. On the one hand, it would seem that left-brained, field independent people are likely to be highly successful at the kinds of language-learning activities we normally find in classrooms. Activities that require analytical skills or the focusing of attention on particular elements of the language, such as a grammatical point or a distinction between sounds, are likely easier for the left-brained learner.

On the other hand, when we look at the whole of the language-learning enterprise, we can see advantages for the field dependent, right-brained learner who may have superior abilities in learning the communicative, social functions of language. Unfortunately, the natural, up-close and personal communication that leads to this kind of learning is fairly rare in the classroom, placing the field dependent learner at a disadvantage in formal learning situations. In a predominantly English-speaking environment that provides ample opportunity for this kind of communication, however, the field dependent learner will thrive.

Is there a contradiction here, then? No, not really. I mentioned earlier that no one is totally dominated by either hemisphere of the brain. Neither is anyone ever totally field dependent or independent; a little of each trait is needed. But it may be important for teachers to recognize which trait is dominant in each learner. It may help to explain why Lucy, for example, excels at classroom language activities and tests but plays quietly by herself on the playground, while Joel muddles through class time and talks a blue streak when he goes out to play. More important, teachers who identify these traits can exploit them as they attempt to individualize their teaching practice.

TOLERANCE OF AMBIGUITY

A third trait that defines individual learning styles is tolerance of ambiguity. In the first university course I taught to graduate students, I presented the arguments for three different theoretical perspectives on language acquisition, each fundamentally different from the others. I painstakingly outlined the case for each position and then the counterarguments. At the end of my carefully prepared lecture, a student put up her hand and asked in frustration, "Well, which one is it? Which one is true?"

Her annoyance reflected more than just a student's quest for truth. It revealed a style of thinking commonly referred to as intolerance of ambiguity. People who see the world in absolute, black-and-white terms, who can't endure uncertainty or ambiguity or who have difficulty accepting, or even understanding, beliefs or practices that run counter to their own, are intolerant of ambiguity. In contrast, people who do not need to have the world packaged into neat bundles of "truth," who see shades of gray mixed in with the black and white, and are relatively open in accepting ideologies that differ from their own are said to be tolerant of ambiguity.

On the surface, it seems that tolerance of ambiguity may be the more desirable trait for successful second language learning. Learners must go through a long period of early learning during which communication itself is extremely uncertain and be able to accept, at least to some degree, the culture that the new language represents. In the English language itself, ambiguity abounds. After all, what is an irregular verb or an irregular plural but a contradiction of the regular inflectional rules? It seems that the ability to deal with conflicting rules, inexplicit or muddled communication and possibly alien ways of viewing the world is a decided advantage.

And it is. On the other hand, though, there is a danger in being excessively tolerant of ambiguity. People who are overly accepting of alternatives, whether in language rules or belief systems, who see only shades of gray and never any black or white, run the risk of being hand-wringers. They're likely to accomplish little because they're unable to take a stand or reject hopeless possibilities. In learning a language, for example, they might accept and memorize each new grammatical rule without regard for apparent contradictions or for its place within an entire rule system. Learners like this might memorize dozens of rules without ever synthesizing them into any kind of internal grammatical system.

I once taught a student who fell into this category. He was so accepting of whatever he was told that he was unable to filter out incorrect information. When other students, barely more proficient than he, gave him their interpretation of a grammatical rule, he accepted it and invested it with as much authority as the rules he encountered in his textbook.

There are also disadvantages, of course, to being excessively intolerant of ambiguity. Not only does a closed mind limit creativity, but learners who are overly intolerant reject behavior that is inconsistent with their own. This behavior might include aspects of the new culture or even the language itself.

So far, research has turned up only a slight advantage for learners who are tolerant of ambiguity, although as Douglas Brown pointed out, the idea that tolerance of ambiguity plays an important role in second language acquisition has intuitive appeal. He said, "It is hard to imagine a compartmentalizer—a person who sees everything in black and white with no shades of gray—ever being successful in the overwhelmingly ambiguous process of learning a second language."

A fourth property of individual learning styles is reflectivity and impulsiveness. Some people weigh each decision in their lives very carefully. They give considerable thought and reflection to each decision they make, no matter how unimportant it may seem to others. As problem-solvers, they tend to be very methodical and calculating, weighing the likely effect of each potential solution.

For example, I have a good friend for whom the buying of a winter coat is a major life event. She begins to think about the coat in August and draws up a list of needs it must meet—warmth during an impending trip to Russia, length to cover the longer skirts she's bought for the winter, a color compatible with most of her clothes but not likely to require constant dry-cleaning, a waterproof shell, perhaps. In September, she begins window shopping, visiting at least ten shops to see what's in stock, the prices, and the likelihood of further stock arriving. By the end of the month, she narrows the list to the four or five stores with the largest selection of coats that meet, or nearly meet, her criteria.

In early October, she refines her list of criteria and begins visiting shops to try on coats. By the end of the month she narrows the contenders to four or five. She then tries on each coat with at least three different outfits that she might wear under it. By November, when two or three of the shortlisted coats have been sold to other customers, she visits more shops and adds new coats to her list. This process continues into December, when it occurs to her that the coats will go on sale in January and she might as well wait. So she does. You can guess what happens. Only one of the original coats is left and she's not sure that it's right her. Besides, winter is half over and she might as well wait until next year! Marjorie is an extremely reflective shopper who hasn't bought a new coat in seven years. I can't imagine her ever buying anything on impulse.

Other people are more impulsive than they are reflective. They tend to make quick, intuitive and somewhat rash decisions. My friend, Ann, is an impulsive thinker and shopper and, needless to say, Marjorie drives her crazy. A visit to Ann's house will tell anyone that she is not a reflective shopper. It's filled with lamps shaped like fire-eating dragons, dinosaur cookie jars, woven chicken baskets in shades of screaming fuchsia and orange, and a rice cooker that plays a song when the rice has finished cooking. All sorts of wondrous things reside in her rooms, none of which could possibly have been bought by a reflective shopper. No, Ann is an impulsive shopper, which is not to say that she is an ineffective one. She does have a winter coat that is not only stylish but also warm.

Shopping is one thing and learning a new language quite another. What might be more relevant to this discussion would be to know how their different thinking styles affect Marjorie and Ann as language learners. I don't have data on that, but what I know about reading suggests that, while Marjorie might read with fewer errors, Ann is likely the faster reader. Studies of the effect of impulsive and reflective thinking on reading have shown that impulsive thinkers make more guesses and more errors in oral reading than reflective thinkers, but their reading comprehension does not seem to be seriously affected.

Although there isn't a great deal of solid research on the effects of either reflectivity or impulsiveness on second language learning, we should nevertheless take the distinction into consideration in our teaching. For example, most classrooms are not equally accepting of reflective and impulsive styles. For the most part, teachers tend to judge harshly the mistakes made by the impulsive thinker who blurts out an answer. We may forget that this is the way this learner thinks things through, works things out.

I have a friend who frequently comes into my office saying things like, "I've decided to go to Pago Pago," or, "I've decided to quit my job and become a carpenter." Of course, he's decided to do neither. He's thinking about it, but this impulse is voiced not because it's the decision he proclaims it to be but because it's his way of thinking aloud. Of course, he is more likely to get on a plane one day and go to Pago Pago to take carpentry lessons than most reflective thinkers. Returning to the classroom, it's easy to see that the child who responds impulsively but incorrectly—to the teacher's way of thinking at least—might be discouraged from progressing through the series of stages that eventually leads her or him to correctness.

It's worth remembering that classrooms aren't always friendly places for reflective thinkers, either. The teacher who is an impulsive thinker may lose patience with the reflective child who needs more time to consider and think about answers before saying them out loud. The real problem may occur because there's a mismatch between the teacher's style and the learner's style, unless the teacher takes special care to recognize that alternative styles may be equally effective. This is not to say that teachers must assess every child to try to uncover his or her precise learning style. Rather, we must be aware of differences that exist within, whether we know their nature or not, and provide a learning environment that is rich and varied enough to provide stimulation for all learners.

Learning styles are, to a large degree, part of the equipment learners bring to the task of learning. We shouldn't, therefore, think about changing or improving on them. Rather, our concern, as teachers, should be to recognize and work with the variety of styles students bring to us. The adaptation required may be as simple as writing down as much as possible of what is said in class or providing an alternative written text that covers essentially the same ground. Doing so recognizes that some students are primarily visual learners while others are primarily aural learners.

## Learning Strategies

As noted earlier, learners also differ in the way they cope with the actual task of learning. They use different learning strategies, which are like blueprints or plans for going about the business of acquiring language. Our current understanding of the role played by strategies in the learning of a language is a result not only of teachers' observations of learners but also of research into learners' intuitions about and insights into their own learning. In fact, some researchers claim that few strategies are actually revealed in classroom observation and that learners' reports on their own strategies are essential to our understanding. In his contribution to *Learner Strategies in Language Learning*, Andrew Cohen observes that interviews with learners are essential if we are to gain meaningful insights into cognitive processing. He also points out the obvious: while learners can report only strategies of which they are conscious, they also almost certainly use strategies of which they are not aware.

No doubt some strategies go unreported either because the elicitation techniques are too clumsy or because learners use metacognitive strategies that are so familiar or habitual that they are unaware of them. Basic strategies like deciding to pay attention to a particular aspect of the language being learned or to monitor one's own pronunciation may go unreported because the learner assumes that everyone does it. For this reason, we'll concentrate here on strategies that have been widely reported and observed to correlate positively with success in language learning.

Although there are many different ways of organizing or categorizing learning strategies, I've chosen to follow the basic division into direct and indirect strategies adopted by Rebecca Oxford in her book *Language Learning Strategies*. Direct strategies are dedicated to dealing with the target language, while indirect strategies are used for managing learning in general.

DIRECT STRATEGIES

In the category of direct strategies, Oxford includes three specific subcategories—memory, cognitive and compensation strategies. Memory strategies are used for remembering and recalling information about the new language. Cognitive strategies are used in the production and comprehension of the new language, and compensation strategies are ways of using the new language even when there are serious gaps in the learner's knowledge of it. Variations in any or all of these strategies can contribute to success or failure in language learning.

Obviously, an important element of language learning is the ability to remember new words, phrases or structures. Some people seem to be especially good at storing and retrieving new language items. Others are not, and tend to write everything down. I've often asked students why they do this. They give the obvious answer—in order to remember it later.

But if these same students are asked to recall an episode of *Murphy Brown* from the previous night or even week, most can recall the gist of the program and possibly even some of the better lines. This isn't because Candice Bergen is funnier than I am but, rather, because of the very existence of the written word. Literacy tends to make our memories lazy. We don't remember because we don't have to. It's written down.

In most circumstances, this isn't cause for concern. In the course of our daily lives, most of us encounter a great deal of information. It's more efficient for us to leave much of it stored away unprocessed, then retrieve it when needed rather than try to commit it all to memory. A statistical formula need not be memorized, for instance, so long as we can remember where to find it. If, in the course of repeated use, we happen to commit it to memory, that's good, but it isn't necessary. When language learning is involved, however, the loss of memory or memorizing strategies may be of great concern because, in nearly all communication situations, learners don't have time to look up the appropriate language items in their notes or dictionaries.

People use different strategies for remembering, and it seems fairly clear that what is effective for one might not be at all effective for another. When I was studying at the University of New Hampshire, a visitor to our teaching English as a second language methods class demonstrated his "Amazing German-Teaching Machine," which was based on the "latest, scientifically respected" principles of auditory memory. The machine, very primitive by today's standards, showed a picture and played the corresponding German word. There was no written word, only the oral. After three repetitions, the machine progressed to the next picture and word. After twenty items had been displayed, the machine presented the items again, this time in a different sequence.

I sat through four complete repetitions for a total of twelve repetitions of each word and learned only two or three words of German. And the way I learned these was to invent a spelling for them and remember that! About two-thirds of my classmates had similar experiences. The others were slightly more successful, though I always suspected that at least some of them already knew German. Clearly, the majority of us who failed to learn the words were neither experienced in nor susceptible to using the auditory memory strategies the machine required.

There are, of course, many possible strategies for remembering. One is to create mental images. Learners who effectively create mental links may do so by grouping language material into meaningful units to make it easier to remember.

Vocabulary, for instance, may be classified according to form (geometric shapes, things with wheels), function (things to ride on, musical instruments), natural categories (mammals, ocean fish) or even feelings (things I hate, colors I like).

Another way to create mental links is to relate new data to what is already stored in memory; that is, by linking new material to existing information or linking new pieces of information to each other. For example, a French speaker learning English might link the English word "lemon" with another new word, "citrus," which corresponds with the French word for lemon, "citron." In this way, the learner has formed two bonds—the two new words, "lemon" and "citrus," to each other and those words to their French cognate.

Still another way of creating a mental link is to place the new word in a context that is meaningful to the learner. Because meaningful material is obviously easier to remember, learners who are able to embed new material in a familiar context are more likely to remember it. Relating words in the new language to similar, or cognate, words in the native language is one way of forming a meaningful mental link between old and new.

Some learners rely on images and sounds to remember language items. In junior high school, I had an English teacher who drew elaborate mental images with words to help us remember irregular spellings. For example, he once described a beautiful little inn nestled somewhere in the Ozark Mountains. He went to great lengths to portray the beauty of the white clapboard building surrounded by brightly colored fall foliage, the neatly lettered green and gold sign hanging on a whitewashed fence, the rooms furnished with antiques and draped with soft velvets. This was, he reminded us, a hotel for honeymooners. It accommodated couples only and, as we wrote the word "accommodate," we were to remember that it, too, accommodated couples—a couple of Cs and a couple of Ms. Creating this image was a lot of effort, but I'm willing to bet that few of my classmates ever misspelled "accommodate."

Semantic mapping, a technique used for a variety of purposes by elementary teachers, is especially useful as a memory aid. To create a semantic map, learners arrange words into a picture that prominently features a key concept or word to which other related words and concepts are joined with lines or arrows. A semantic map for the word "forest," for example, might look something like this:

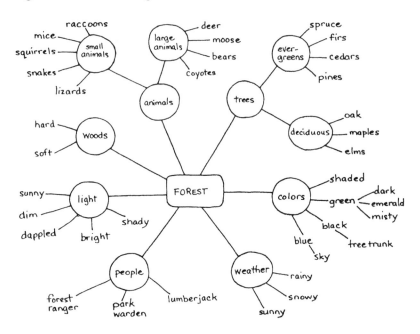

 Rebecca Oxford lists two further strategies within the general sub-category of applying images and sounds—using key words and representing sounds in memory. To use the first, learners form an auditory link by identifying a word in the first language that sounds like the word in the target language. Then they generate a visual link between the two. For example, the Chinese word for noodle, "mein," sounds like the English word "mane." Manes are composed of long strands of hair and noodles are made up of long strands of dough. Thus, both an auditory and a visual link are created and "mein" is remembered. Like using cognate words, this strategy involves linking new information to old.

The strategy of representing sounds in memory consists of activating a broad array of auditory recall methods. For instance, learners may associate a new word with a word in another language or even with a non-language sound. The word for bread in Chinese, "bao," might be linked with the sound a dog makes or the words "bough" or "bow."

Organized reviewing is another simple but effective strategy used by many learners. Most of us probably employed this strategy at one time or another with at least some success during our school or university careers. It entails carefully reviewing the newly learned material at regularly spaced intervals over and over again until it becomes routine. The disadvantage of this strategy for language learners is that it's extremely time-consuming and is ineffective when a great deal of language material is involved.

A further memory strategy links physical activity with the act of remembering. The activity may be as simple as writing a new word on a card or list and then moving the card to a new pile or crossing the word off the list once it's learned. Or it may be a more complicated bodily maneuver. Total physical response is a language-teaching approach that relies heavily on this strategy. Learners first respond physically to an instructor's commands such as, "Stand up," "Sit down," "Open the window," and "Raise your book into the air." James Asher, who pioneered TPR, believes that linking physical activity with verbal stimuli increases the likelihood that the learner will remember the new language.

Undoubtedly, learners use more than one memory strategy with differing degrees of success. It is perhaps stating the obvious to suggest that when it comes to remembering language—or anything else, for that matter—what works for some people will seem clumsy and ineffectual to others. Nevertheless, it's essential for language learners, especially those faced with the monumental task of learning English vocabulary, to develop memory strategies that work for them.

Proficient language learners are active participants in their own learning. We use the term cognitive strategy to refer to the ways they manipulate language data to make it more "learnable" as they're learning it. Like memory strategies, cognitive strategies vary greatly from learner to learner. There is also a great deal of variation in what writers and researchers identify as cognitive strategies. H. Douglas Brown, for instance, lists fourteen while Rebecca Oxford lists fifteen and Anna Chamot twelve. The seven on which all three agree are repetition, note-taking, referring to resources, translation, transfer, recombination and deduction.

Repetition, saying or writing the same item over and over, is a time-honored tradition among language learners. It's built into most teaching methods and appeals to our intuitions about what we need to do in order to learn. Most of us will intuitively repeat or write a new word several times immediately after hearing it. A student of Japanese, for example, might learn the syllabic writing system by repeating the syllable over and over while simultaneously forming the appropriate strokes on paper. Repetition is a strategy that most learners don't need to be taught and is effective so long as it isn't used to the exclusion of all other strategies or to the point that it becomes boring. Left to their own devices, most learners will abandon the strategy once it's no longer needed.

Note-taking is a good example of active participation because, if it's used effectively, the learner must select from and summarize rather than reproduce exactly what's presented. While most students have some note-taking experience, they aren't all efficient or effective note-takers. Teachers can do much to help learners develop this skill, an effective cognitive learning strategy.

Although it's an essential strategy, note-taking is not appropriate or effective in all situations. Sometimes learners must use outside resources to make sense of a message. These resources may be reference materials in the target language or non-print materials such as pictures, drawings or figures. When a learner asks a native speaker of a language to explain the meaning of a word or idiom, this too is referring to an outside resource.

In the early stages of language learning, learners frequently resort to the first language as a means of understanding or making sense of the target language. This kind of translation may work in either direction; that is, learners may convert target language utterances into the native language or native language utterances into the target language. As a beginning strategy, this may be effective. Certainly, several million Chinese speakers have learned English using methods based largely on translation.

As a long-term strategy or for developing an advanced level of competence in the language, however, translation is inefficient and counterproductive. Too many processing steps are required when learners translate everything they hear into their own language, formulate a response and then translate it back into English. Communication would be as slow and unnatural as it is when sequential translation is used in international meetings. To become fully proficient in a new language, learners must eventually abandon translation as a strategy and begin to think as much as possible in the target language.

Transfer is a strategy related to translation. When learners take advantage of previously learned language material by applying it to a new language situation, they are transferring their knowledge. Transfer is a powerful strategy, even though learners may not be aware that they're using it. In fact, it's nearly impossible to avoid transfer in the early stages of learning a new language because learners must call upon all their available resources to understand and learn. These resources include what they've already learned about how languages work. For example, they may know that word order differs between the two languages, giving them a peg to hang the new concept on. An English speaker studying French, then, may know that the usual order of noun modification in French is noun-adjective and remember this by making up the rule, Reverse the order of adjective and noun in French. This rule, of course, doesn't always apply and, one day, it won't be needed any longer. Nevertheless, as a beginning strategy, it works more often than not.

Many of us who studied another language in high school had direct experience with the strategy of recombination, especially when it's combined with memorization. More than twenty-five years later, I still recall learning the sentence, "Pauline Adams est une jeune étudiante Américaine." Needless to say, even at that time, my French teacher knew that it was extremely unlikely that any of us would ever need to utter this particular sentence. To prepare us for related needs, however, he taught us to substitute new items in the familiar frame—Pauline became Genevieve and, later, Susan, aged a few years, and was at various times French, German and Italian. She apparently graduated at some point because we started to talk about her in the past tense. Since then, I've often been aware of using the same strategy—learning a useful sentence frame, then combining parts of it with new language items to form a more useful expression.

We use a similar strategy when we try to comprehend a new language. Teachers often use a familiar "frame" to introduce new words or ideas, sometimes relying on another strategy, such as referring to other resources or guessing, discussed later in this section, to make the meaning clear. My Chinese teacher, for example, began lessons with the question, "Ni hao ma?" and taught us to respond by saying, "Hen hao." Later, when I was in China, I heard an English friend express dissatisfaction with something by saying, "Bu hao."

The common element in all these expressions, together with the context, helped me make sense of them. "Hao" refers to a state of being, akin to "well" in English. My teacher's question—"How are you?" or "Are you well?"—drew the response, "Very well," or, more literally, "Positive well." "Bu," as I was quick to learn, is a negative and so "bu hao" meant "not well" or "not good."

Deductive reasoning is another widely used and effective cognitive strategy. It occurs when learners apply general rules they have learned to new language situations. For example, the beginning student of Chinese who learns that the word "ma" signals a question can apply this knowledge to form questions, provided that she or he has some other knowledge of Chinese sentences.

A common example of deductive thinking, and one that is somewhat controversial in first language pedagogy, is the use of phonics rules. Learners who are struggling to decode the English sound system in written text often find that a simple phonics rule is a great asset. For instance, students faced with the list of words, "seeing," "sealing" and "ceiling," might correctly identify the same vowel sound in all of them if they're equipped with the simple schoolroom rhyme, When two vowels go walking, the first one does the talking. Unfortunately—and this is one source of the controversy—the rule is useless when it comes to encoding or spelling and it is often broken (e.g., "oo" is pronounced differently in "mood" and "hood," and "lead" sometimes rhymes with "bed"). Nevertheless, because it works about 44 per cent of the time, it's generally conceded to be better than nothing for beginning readers, especially when it's combined with a compensation strategy.

Proficient language learners are usually good at guessing and figuring things out from situational and other contexts. Because compensation strategies like these seem to be needed only when learners haven't yet learned enough language to communicate their intended meaning, it may seem odd to talk about them at this point. However, they are important to the learning process. By helping learners communicate successfully, thus gaining experience in using the target language, they give a significant boost to language learning. Compensation strategies, then, enable students to use the new language despite significant gaps in their knowledge or proficiency.

Educated guessing is a highly effective compensation strategy. Even as proficient readers of English, many of us guess at meaning when we encounter a new word or phrase in an otherwise familiar text. Doing this is faster than looking up every unfamiliar word, especially if we happen to be reading in a train station or other locale where a dictionary isn't readily available. It's also less intrusive, and possibly more reliable, than asking other people who happen to be nearby. Research has shown that proficient language learners guess at meaning, while less able learners panic or try to look up every unknown word.

Guessing, one of the strategies taught in the English for academic purposes courses at the TESL Centre at Saint Mary's University, improves reading speed and comprehension as well as students' ability to listen effectively. Beginning with written text and proceeding to speech, we first demonstrate techniques for working out the meaning of words or passages by thinking aloud about or talking our way through a problematic text. We then guide individual students through the process, asking them questions when necessary to elicit things they already know that may be helpful. When combined with training in note-taking, this technique produces better comprehension and a higher confidence level in learners.

Compensation strategies used when speaking and writing are necessarily different from those used when reading and listening. Guessing is less effective when speaking and writing, but learners can be taught to use other strategies to help compensate for their lack of knowledge. For example, they may be encouraged to substitute a word from another language for one they don't know in English. There is always a chance that their audience, whether listeners or readers, will know the other language or recognize what is meant from the context and supply the correct English word. Similarly, if a student uses a word that is similar, though not exactly the same, in meaning, a listener will sometimes offer the appropriate term. In this way, the compensation strategy becomes a learning as well as a communication strategy.

Two other compensation strategies deserve mention because they are, in my experience, widely used when children are learning a second language. One is to coin or make up a new word to express the intended meaning. A young Vietnamese girl I once knew came up with "fluest" to describe the seriousness of her cold when she had to stay home from school. Another is to control the topic. I've often seen adult students at the TESL Centre employ this strategy at social functions where the topics of conversation tend to be rather diverse. One of them, an Iranian man, was very quiet in class, yet at receptions he became the life of the party, talking to everyone for a little while and never hesitating to bring up a new subject of conversation. When I commented that he seemed to enjoy these functions, he took exception, assuring me that he found them very hard work. When I pointed out that he could stand quietly for at least part of the time if he found it easier, he told me that this would be even more stressful. He explained that if he introduced the topic, he could be reasonably certain of possessing the necessary vocabulary to carry on a conversation. Otherwise, he ran the risk of someone bringing up a subject like football or hockey that he knew very little about. In a sense, this tactic amounted to avoidance. But it's more productive than avoidance because it involved the young man in conversation during which he undoubtedly learned more English.

INDIRECT STRATEGIES

The strategies we've examined so far have been directly associated with language learning. In computer terminology, we would say that they are "dedicated" to the specific task of learning a language. They are, however, supported by a more general set of strategies for managing all the learning an individual does. These are indirect strategies and include three general categories—metacognitive, affective and social strategies.

"Metacognitive" is an odd word, one whose meaning is not immediately obvious even though we may understand its components—"meta," meaning "beyond" and "cognitive," referring to mental or intellectual processes. When we use the term, however, we aren't talking about something outside the realm of cognition. Rather, we're talking about processes that transcend the cognitive processes or strategies described earlier. As Rebecca Oxford put it, "Metacognitive strategies are actions which go beyond purely cognitive devices, and which provide a way for learners to coordinate their own learning process."

Writers vary in the number of metacognitive strategies they identify. For example, Anna Chamot lists eight while Rebecca Oxford lists only three. Because these three are general enough to include nearly all those on the longer list, however, I will use her classification here. They are centering of learning, arranging and planning learning, and evaluating learning.

Centering learning refers in large part to focus and attention. A centered learner has decided in advance to ignore irrelevant distractions and pay attention to the learning task at hand. This may apply to general tasks, such as enrolling in and attending a language class, or specific tasks, such as focusing on a specific aspect of language. For instance, the centered learner may decide to concentrate on listening rather than speaking, focusing attention on this aspect of language and leaving speaking practice to another time. The learner may further focus the learning experience by reviewing previously learned material in an effort to find the appropriate "place" for material about to be learned.

Proficient language learners use a number of effective strategies to arrange and plan their learning experiences. Using advance organizers works well for many people. This entails doing a general overview of what is to be learned to discover the organizing concept or principle. Effective teachers often provide advance organizers for students, whether this is a formal outline or less formal introductory remarks such as, "Today, we'll examine three different ways of expressing future time. The first is the most commonly used."

Another planning strategy is to set goals and objectives. At the TESL Centre, we train students to set their own goals and objectives at the beginning of each class after the organizing principle for the lesson has been introduced and discussed. We also encourage them to establish specific goals for their study sessions at home.

It's important for learners to have a sense of how successful they are at meeting their goals and, generally, of their own progress. While some indication of achievement can come from the teacher, learners must find ways to monitor and evaluate their own learning if they are to become independent. At some time or other, we've probably all experienced the frustration of having our learning assessed unfairly, at least to our way of thinking. The age-old lament of students—"If only she'd asked what I knew"—isn't entirely unreasonable.

Tests, whether devised by the teacher or at a testing center, measure only part of what any learner knows and, while they may be entirely fair in assessing progress in comparison with earlier test results or the results of other people, they rarely measure absolute achievement. Most students learn a great deal that is never measured by tests. External evaluation, then, can leave them feeling frustrated and unnerved. This makes it essential, therefore, for them to learn to evaluate their own progress. For example, it's fairly easy for students to tell whether they're reading faster than they were a month or two earlier and whether they're understanding and making themselves understood better than at some earlier time. The wise teacher encourages students to make these judgments for themselves because doing so builds confidence and independence.

Affective strategies refer to the ways we deal with the emotions, attitudes, values and motivations that might influence our learning. Affective strategies are extremely important because, as Rebecca Oxford pointed out, "Good language learners are often those who know how to control their emotions and attitudes about learning."

One commonly used affective strategy is to lower our anxiety level. For example, I've observed students take a few minutes to meditate before beginning an examination, and I know a Chinese student who routinely went to an afternoon movie before writing an evening examination. I've taught other students to do deep-breathing exercises as a way of relaxing and opening their minds to the learning task at hand. In all cases, the aim has been to lower their anxiety levels, thereby enhancing their learning potential.

A second affective strategy is self-encouragement. I've heard graduate students give themselves pep talks before writing examinations or giving seminar presentations. Similarly, ESL students sometimes give themselves small rewards for a good performance in class or on a paper or examination. Teachers, of course, can help students find ways both to lower their anxiety levels and encourage themselves but, in the end, learners must take charge of their own emotions, attitudes and motivation if they are to learn independently and success-fully.

Students must also learn to monitor their own attitudes and feelings about the business of learning. If they are to do anything about them, they must learn to recognize negative attitudes or the causes of low motivation. Teachers can assist in this process in a variety of ways. One of these is to initiate a dialogue journal in which we might gently probe the reasons students are experiencing negative feelings about their own learning.

STRATEGY RETRAINING

Unlike learning styles, which are intrinsic to learners and unlikely to change, learning strategies can be changed. Indeed, we're talking about an area in which change is not only possible, but may also be desirable. Teachers can have a major impact on this, though it isn't always easy to persuade learners to abandon ineffective or counterproductive strategies.

Students may be extremely reluctant to give up strategies that worked in the past for a different kind of learning or in a different situation, even when faced with the evidence that they are no longer working. For instance, I've seen Chinese students in Canada valiantly translating page after page of an English novel into Chinese and memorizing pages of dialogue from ESL textbooks. Their subsequent difficulties in communicating with native English speakers are predictable from our point of view, but frustrating for them. Frustrating and surprising, because these methods were very successful in China—under different circumstances and when the language was being learned for different purposes.

Strategy retraining may play an important role, then, in teaching children, especially those who attended school before emigrating to an English-speaking country. The point isn't that they have learned to learn badly, for this almost certainly isn't the case. Rather, their old strategies might not be as effective when they encounter a particular language-learning task in a new setting.

Teachers may need to work at identifying ineffective strategies and helping students learn more successful ones. It may be a good idea to start with affective strategies because learners who feel positive about the learning task and their ability to learn will be more receptive to making the other adjustments that may be required. Teachers who wish to know more about learning strategies and effective exercises for strategy retraining might refer to *Learner Strategies in Language Learning*, edited by Anita Wenden and Joan Rubin, and Rebecca Oxford's *Language Learning Strategies*. For practical suggestions in strategy training, see the series, *Building Bridges: Content and Learning Strategies for ESL*, by Anna Chamot, J. Michael O'Malley and Lisa Kupper.

## LANGUAGES THEY KNOW AND

## THE LANGUAGE THEY LEARN

For the past twenty-three years, I've taught English to learners from more than twenty different countries. Whatever their native language, these learners had a common complaint about English: it's hard to learn. As someone who has failed at learning several languages, I'm tempted to claim that this is true because *all* languages are difficult to learn. But, in fact, English is an especially complicated language.

A particularly observant learner from China summed up the problem this way, "English is a strange language. There must be at least a million words but, with all these words, you still use the same word to mean lots of different things." When he said this, my friend, Mao Dawei, spoke more truth than he knew. English does have a lot of words. Some estimates run as high as a million, although the exact number is impossible to calculate. New words are constantly being added, while others fall into disuse and the meaning of still others is modified. And how do we count words? Are "dog" and "dogs" two separate words? Are the verb and adjective forms of words such as "clear" or the noun and verb forms of "dust" counted separately? Then, there's Mao's point about all the words that look and sound the same but have different meanings. "Bear," for example, means one thing as a noun and quite another as a verb.

Dictionaries aren't much help in solving the problem. The *Oxford Dictionary of Current English* has between 70,000 and 75,000 entries while *Webster's Third New International Dictionary of the English Language*, published in 1966, lists 450,000 words. Because we can be sure that the vocabulary of English hasn't shrunk in the years since and because many thousands of technical words associated with fields like medicine and law aren't included in dictionaries, we can safely assume that this is a conservative estimate. Besides, as we all know, not all the words we hear or use are found in the dictionary.

Perhaps a more relevant estimate of vocabulary, then, is the number of words English speakers know. In general, this number is underestimated. Textbook writers and educators commonly assume that high school graduates recognize about 50,000 words, even though they may use only 10,000 or so in their speaking and writing. Karl Diller showed that high school students, in fact, recognize more than 200,000 words, while university professors know approximately 250,000.

English has such an extensive vocabulary because it has borrowed rather freely from the languages of the various invaders of England over the centuries. By the time Old English was spoken, between 450 and 1100, it had already been influenced by Celtic, Latin and Germanic languages. Over the next four centuries, it borrowed from the Scandinavian languages and very heavily from French. Latin and Greek continued to loan words to English through the next several centuries and, with the development of American English, new influences began to appear. All this borrowing has not only left English with a massive vocabulary, but it has also made it similar in many ways to a number of other languages.

When non-native speakers begin to learn English, they marshal all their available resources. One of these is their knowledge of their own language. If their language is German or another Germanic language, there will be certain obvious similarities because Old English and Old High German are from the same family. If their language is French or any of the Latinate languages, it will have certain other similarities to English because French had a major impact on English as a result of the Norman Conquest. But there will be differences as well. German and English haven't been the same for more than 1,000 years and, over the centuries, each has changed in vastly different ways. Similarly, English was already well-established at the time of the Norman Conquest and was never completely dominated by Norman French.

Naturally, it's the differences between languages that worry learners, creating, to their way of thinking at least, major obstacles to success. While this problem is exaggerated, it's true that transfer from one language to another does occur, producing certain kinds of errors. It's useful for us as teachers to understand why some of the more common transfer errors occur, not so we can prevent them but so we can make informed decisions about how to correct them. In this chapter, then, we'll look at English as it's seen by many ESL learners and highlight some of the differences that are likely to cause transfer problems. Then, we'll conclude with a note on the role transfer plays in children's learning.

## English and the Languages They Know

Clearly, the purpose of this book isn't to describe fully the structure of English. Many excellent books offer detailed descriptions of this. Nevertheless, we'll examine how differences between English and some other languages are likely to affect the learning of English.

SOUND SYSTEMS

To most people, what distinguishes one language from another is the way it sounds. French doesn't sound like English, German or Italian, while Chinese doesn't sound like Korean or Japanese. This isn't simply because of the obvious fact that these languages have different words, that "chapeau" sounds different from "hat" or "cap," or that the Chinese word for "chicken" is "ji." Sitting in a crowded restaurant or airport where many people are talking, we can frequently identify the languages spoken even though we can't quite hear, or can hear but not understand, the words.

My Chinese friends have often remarked that my attempts at Chinese sound like some other language—not English, but certainly not Chinese. A colleague of mine, on the other hand, is expert at mimicking the sounds of Chinese and, indeed, almost any language he hears, although he doesn't know any Chinese words. It is more than word differences, then, that distinguish the sound systems of different languages.

If we think about the sounds of English from the perspective of non-native speakers attempting to learn them, we begin to understand the complexity of the system. First, they must learn to make the individual sounds of the twenty-four consonants and fifteen vowels, including diphthongs, that make up English. Complicating this task is the fact that every speaker of English utters each sound a little differently and, furthermore, utters the sounds slightly differently when saying different words. In fact, there are one or two fewer distinctive vowels in some English dialects. Most Canadians, for example, use the same vowel sound when saying "pot" and "father."

Learners must figure out which sounds are distinctive and how much variation they can safely ignore. In learning this, they must also learn that some sounds change character in different combinations. For example, the English sound /k/ is articulated slightly differently in the words "king," "cat," and "score." For many learners, differences like this aren't problematic, but for others they are.

*Distinctive Sounds*

In English, many pairs of words differ by only one sound. These are called minimal pairs and they're useful because they demonstrate to non-native speakers which sounds are distinctive. For example, if we look at the words "pill," "bill" and "gill," we can see that the sounds /p/, /b/ and /g/ are distinctive because substituting one for the other changes the meaning.

If we then compare "pill" and "poll," "bill" and "bowl" and "gill" and "goal," we see that the two vowel sounds, /I/ and /o/, are also distinctive.

These examples also demonstrate how each sound may have several possible and permissible pronunciations. We pronounce the /g/ in "gill," for example, just a little differently from the same sound in "goal." Substituting the /g/ sound in "gill" for that in "goal," or vice versa, results in a distorted pronunciation that sounds strange to the native speaker but doesn't change the meaning.

*Distinctive Sounds in Other languages*

Languages differ dramatically in the number of distinctive sounds used to convey meaning. Some Polynesian languages, for instance, have as few as a dozen distinctive sounds. Remember that English has more vowels than that. On the other hand, the Khosian language !Xu has twenty-four vowels and 117 consonants.

Because it's unlikely that many of us will encounter more than one or two !Xu speakers in our lifetimes, however, I'll confine my examples to the languages more commonly spoken by the learners we're likely to encounter. Spanish, for example, has only five vowels and five diphthongs, while the vowels in German are quite similar to those of English. It is the English consonants that cause Germans more problems, in part because English has certain sounds, such as /b/, /v/ and /z/, that either don't occur at all in German or occur in different environments.

*Environmental Change*

In English, as indeed in all languages, sounds behave differently in different environments. This natural variation occurs because speech consists not of the precise articulation of individual sounds but of a more fluid blending of sounds. The sounds immediately surrounding an individual sound will, then, affect its actual pronunciation.

Native speakers of English are accustomed to this variation and scarcely notice it. For non-native learners, however, some of these variants are especially problematic. One example of this variation occurs frequently in English and is puzzling to many non-English speakers. It's called vowel reduction and occurs because we pronounce a vowel one way when it's stressed and another way when it isn't. Consider the differences in the pronunciation of the boldface vowel in the following pairs of words:

minor—minority
ridicule—ridiculous
grammar—grammatical

These differences are caused by the change in stress that occurs when a suffix is added. Vowel reduction, however, happens so commonly in English during normal or rapid speech that it sometimes appears that a single vowel sound, the schwa (/ə/), is the most important in the language. When we consider the vowel sounds in the sentence, "The runner was stopped by a number of dusty, thirsty persons," we discover that twelve of the sixteen are schwas, although those followed by "r" may sound slightly different.

The fact that these vowels are spelled differently and, indeed, pronounced differently in different circumstances often causes confusion among non-native speakers. Spanish, Italian and Portuguese speakers often complain that English words are hard to understand because English vowels all sound the same.

As complex as they are, however, English vowel sounds cause learners less trouble than the consonants. Vowels seem to be easier to learn. It's possible that this is because there are fewer vowels than consonants, something that is true in all languages. More likely, however, it's because of inherent acoustic properties that make them easier to perceive than consonants. Specifically, vowels are all voiced—the vocal chords vibrate as the sounds are pronounced—and highly resonant because the airstream is not impeded in the oral cavity as each is produced. Lending credibility to this argument is the empirical evidence that child ESL learners make fewer errors with vowels than with consonants.

Contributing to the difficulty of learning consonants is the fact that their pronunciation often deviates according to their context. An example is the English /r/. As we saw earlier, even though we tend to think of /r/ as a single sound, it is actually pronounced in many different ways depending on the context. Consider carefully how the tongue and lips are positioned to pronounce the /r/ sound in each of the following words:

| bark | rich | grand |
| bird | row | tree |

It's difficult for native speakers to imagine how different these sounds seem to foreign learners because we spell them with the same symbol and have come to perceive them as the same. But, acoustically, the "r" in "bark" bears a closer resemblance to the "l" in "balk" than to the "r" in "ripple." No wonder the English sound system is hard to master!

The way individual sounds or features of these sounds are distributed, then, marks a crucial difference between languages. In Vietnamese, for example, aspiration is distinctive. To illustrate, let's consider how we pronounce certain words in English. In words that begin with voiceless stops—sounds, such as /p/, /t/ and /k/, that are pronounced without vibrating the vocal chords—these sounds are usually followed by a tiny puff air known as an aspiration. Thus, the initial consonants in "pill," "kiss," and "tall" are produced as /p$^h$/, /k$^h$/ and /t$^h$/ respectively. This isn't true when the same consonants appear at the ends of words or syllables. In contrast, Vietnamese distinguishes between aspirated and unaspirated /t/. The unaspirated /t/ is usually spelled with a "d" that to the English speaker's ear sounds like a /d/ even though it isn't voiced. Vietnamese also has a heavily aspirated "th," spelled "th."

Another example of the way the same sounds may be distributed differently in two languages is found if we compare Greek and English. Both /s/ and /z/ are distinctive phonemes in Greek and English. In Greek, however, only /z/ appears before /m/, and thus Greek speakers learning English will often say "zmile" for "smile" or "zmell" for "smell." A further example is found in Japanese, which doesn't distinguish between /l/ and /r/. Thus Japanese learners have trouble both hearing and producing this important distinction in English.

*Syllable Structure*

ESL teachers are aware that certain sounds are more difficult than others. Sometimes, though, it is neither the vowels nor the consonants nor even the distribution of these sounds that causes trouble so much as the syllable structure of English.

Because syllables are structured differently in different languages, second language learners sometimes transfer the syllabic configurations from their native language to English. English permits a great many combinations of sounds in its syllables. As illustrated here, English syllables may begin with either a vowel or a consonant and contain a variety of sound patterns:

V—Vowel Sound    C—Consonant Sound

Syllables beginning with vowels:

V—oh
VC—am
VCC—ant
VCCC—inks

Syllables beginning with consonants:

CV—be
CCV—tree
CCCV—stray
CVC—bet
CCVC—treat
CCCVC—stream
CVCC—bets
CCVCC—treats
CCCVCC—streets
CVCCC—desks
CCVCCC—grinds
CCCVCCC—strands
CVCCCC—texts

The variety of syllable structures permitted in English causes problems with both production and comprehension. Learners have trouble both pronouncing some consonant clusters and determining where word boundaries lie—where one word ends and another begins, especially when speech is rapid. Those familiar with less complicated syllabic structures experience particular problems with English. In Italian, for example, consonants appear infrequently at the end of syllables. This is why Italian ESL students sometimes produce sentences such as, "He wenta to schoola ona Monday."

Similarly, Chinese speakers are unaccustomed to consonants other than nasals in the final position in words. In Chinese, syllables normally consist of a consonant followed by a vowel only or a vowel and /m/ or /n/. Thus, Chinese learners may correctly pronounce words such as "ring," "run" and "same" but drop—or fail to produce—the final sounds in words such as "bat," "frog," "rib" and "duck."

As native speakers, we have no difficulty with words such as "strip," which has a CCCVC structure—three consonants followed by a vowel and another consonant—or "sprint," which has a CCVCC structure. For native Chinese speakers, however, these are especially difficult words, and they may "regularize" their pronunciation by placing a schwa between the consonants, producing "puh-lain" for "plain" or "guh-rim" for "grim." Japanese speakers have similar problems with English consonant clusters and their solution is often the same—to insert a vowel sound between consonant clusters.

This process yields words such as "bes-i-boru" for "baseball." Vietnamese, Thai, Turkish, Farsi, Portuguese, Spanish and Arabic speakers also have problems with English consonant clusters because the range of possible clusters is much more restricted in those languages. Dutch and German speakers, on the other hand, tend to experience fewer problems because their languages have similar syllabic structures.

*Prosodic features*

Learners who have mastered pronunciation of the individual sounds of English, the slight changes in sound that occur in different environments, and the way sounds combine in syllables have gone a long way toward mastering the sound system. But not all the way. They must also learn the stress and intonation patterns that give English its characteristic rhythm, its "Englishness." These are as important to learners' ability to make themselves understood as any of the other features of the sound system.

Earlier, I cited the example of the crowded airport to illustrate how important sound is in differentiating languages. Let's go back to the airport for a moment and imagine that two people are talking at a table a few feet away from us. They aren't speaking loudly enough for us to make out the individual words. We have no idea what they're talking about, but there is no doubt that they're speaking English. At another table, a family is engaged in animated conversation. Again, although the words are inaudible, we can say with confidence that they're speaking French.

What helps us make these judgments is the characteristic "melody"—the prosodic features—of the language. Generally speaking, the prosodic features of language include variations in pitch (or tone), loudness and speed or rhythm. For the most part, native English speakers use pitch to indicate a wide range of meanings. For example, we might distinguish between statements and questions by varying our pitch, or intonation, in sentences such as, "Herbie has gone," and "Herbie has gone?"

In contrast, tone or pitch changes in more than half the world's languages occur at the word level and mark distinctions in word meaning. In Chinese, a language with four tones, the tonal quality of the vowel signals significant differences in meaning. For instance, the word "mai" can mean "to buy" or "to sell." When spoken with a falling-rising tone, it means "to buy," but when spoken with a falling tone, it means "to sell." Some Chinese words have four different meanings depending on the tone used.

Vietnamese is even more complicated—six distinctive tones can affect meaning. On a recent trip to Vietnam, I managed to order poison beer rather than three bottles of beer by merely getting the tone on "ba" wrong. There were at least four other mistakes I could have made with the same syllable, but none of them was quite so dangerous. Fortunately, the context saved the day and my life. I was ordering for my two companions and myself, and the waiter explained that while he thought it possible that I might wish to poison my friends, he considered it highly unlikely that I'd want to do in myself as well. Obviously, his English was better than my Vietnamese!

Changes in loudness or volume also affect meaning. By altering the loudness of an utterance in English, we can do things like emphasize its importance, indicate that it's confidential or convey anger. Altering volume at the syllable level also helps speakers convey emphasis and words may be stressed by changing both tone and volume.

For those of us who've always spoken English, applying stress to our utterances seems quite natural. But think about it for a minute. Every word has its own characteristic stress. In polysyllabic words, one syllable is always stressed more than the others. In "reply," "deny" and "descend," for example, the second syllable is stressed more heavily than the first. In "quarterly," "indigo," and "desperate," the first syllable is stressed more heavily than the other two. This assignment of stress is totally arbitrary, meaning that there are no rules governing it.

ESL learners frequently have difficulty with English stress patterns. English is a stress-timed language, meaning that stressed syllables occur at roughly regular intervals and are interspersed with unstressed syllables. French, in contrast, is a syllable-timed language, meaning that the syllables are produced in a steady flow. French speakers who apply French stress patterns to English produce a staccato effect that is more typical of French than English.

Speakers of tonal languages, those in which the pitch of a word is used to distinguish differences in meaning, sometimes experience similar problems but for different reasons. Stressed English syllables are articulated with a slightly higher pitch or tone than unstressed syllables. Speakers of tonal languages often have trouble indicating stress with a change in tone because they're used to a system in which a change in tone causes a change in meaning. As a result, they tend to pronounce polysyllabic words with full stress on each syllable, producing an unnaturally staccato effect.

In some cases, Vietnamese and Chinese learners try to stress syllables by increasing only the volume and not the pitch. Several years ago, I met a Vietnamese man whose English was almost unintelligible even though he'd been studying English in Canada for more than a year. His pronunciation of individual sounds was fairly accurate, but his sentences were almost impossible to comprehend. When I listened carefully, I discovered that he was making two crucial errors. First, he was stressing far more syllables than necessary. Second, although he was varying the stress on words somewhat, his method of producing stress was simply to increase the volume without raising the pitch. It took several months of "ear" training before his pronunciation began to improve.

Stress, pitch and tempo all contribute to the rhythm of a language. The louder volume, higher pitch and longer vowels of stressed syllables give us the "beat" that we can tap out as we say phrases or sentences. Pitch is central to some Oriental tonal languages, giving each its unique melody. It takes very little experience, for example, for an English speaker to hear the difference between Mandarin Chinese with its four tones and Cantonese with its six.

## Spelling and Pronunciation

If languages weren't written, we could all go about learning them without worrying about bothersome details like spelling. But they are written and those, like English, that are only roughly phonetic cause problems in both spelling and pronunciation.

The relationship between the written and the spoken word varies from language to language. The English writing system is roughly phonetic—its symbols represent individual speech sounds. On the other hand, the Chinese writing system is logographic—the symbols represent words or ideas. Its graphemes identify meaning without conveying information about pronunciation. Most of the world's languages, however, are, like English, alphabetic and phonetic, with a more or less predictable relationship between the way a word is spelled and the way it's pronounced. In Greek, this relationship is almost perfect; in English it's extremely tenuous. Spanish, Italian, French, Dutch, German and Vietnamese fall somewhere in between.

Speakers of languages with more predictable sound-symbol relationships than English often experience frustration when reading and writing this language. Having learned how "tough" and "rough" are pronounced, for example, they are then confronted with "dough" and "though." They really lose patience when they come up against the dual pronunciations of words such as "read" and "lead." For children, however, this problem is not as severe as it is with older learners. They've had less time to develop firm expectations about how words should sound, if they've learned to read at all, and are more accepting of the anomalies of English spelling.

## WORDS

Of course, there is more to learning a language than mastering its pronunciation. Students must learn the words of a language, a task that includes understanding how morphemes combine to form words and create meaning. Morphemes are the smallest units of meaning in a language and morphology refers to the study of word structure, the way these units are combined to form words. The morphological structure of various languages differs radically.

From the time they begin to learn English, learners are aware of its lexical morphemes, the units that carry the burden of meaning. Many, such as "baby," "ball," and "shoe," stand alone as words. Other morphemes may be attached to them, however, changing their meaning (e.g., "babyfaced," "softball" and "shoeless"). Although most meaning-carrying morphemes can stand alone, a few, called bound morphemes, must be attached to other morphemes to form words. Examples include "bio-," meaning "life," "photo-," meaning "light," and "ante-," meaning "before."

Second language learners, however, must learn much more than the lexical morphemes to understand how word meanings are created in English. By learning its derivational morphemes, they discover that adding certain kinds of morphemes to certain classes of words creates new uses for these words. For instance, the word "murk" is rarely used. But when the morpheme "-y" is added, forming "murky," it becomes much more useful. This suffix can be added to a whole class of nouns to form adjectives, increasing the accuracy and communicative capacity of a learner's speech.

Unfortunately for the learner, this "rule" isn't as straightforward as simply adding "-y" to nouns to form adjectives. First, not all nouns can be turned into adjectives this way—for example, we can't say "computery" or "booky." Second, the same /i/ sound that turns nouns into adjectives also turns adjectives, such as "full," into adverbs, such as "fully."

Learning inflections, the affixes that signal grammatical relationships, is another important aspect of acquiring English. Inflectional morphemes don't have much intrinsic meaning, but they carry a great deal of information that is important to the correct interpretation of sentences. English has seven inflectional morphemes, most of which have two or three different phonetic varieties as indicated on this chart:

| Inflection | Phonetic Forms | Examples |
|---|---|---|
| Past Tense | /t/, /d/ /əd/ and irregulars | stamped, canned, dusted, ran |
| Present Progressive Tense | -ing | rising, falling |
| Third Person Singular | /s/, /z/ | walks, runs, wishes |
| Plural | /s/, /z/, /əz/ and irregulars | cats, dogs, horses, mice |
| Possessive | /s/, /z/, /əz/ | Jack's, Jane's, Bush's |
| Comparative | /ər/, more | richer, more intelligent |
| Superlative | /ɛst/, most | brightest, most productive |

Fortunately, English inflections are relatively straightforward for speakers of languages such as French, which has a more complicated system of inflections, especially of the verb. Chinese learners, on the other hand, find this system difficult because there are no inflections at all in either Mandarin or Cantonese. At first, all learners simplify English by omitting at least some of these grammatical "frills," but Chinese learners may persist a little longer because the inflectional process is so alien to them.

*Other Word Formation Processes*

To master English fully, learners must be able to combine words to form compounds, a process that appears straightforward. For example, "chair" and "person" combine to form "chairperson," the person who chairs a meeting. And a "milkman" is the man who delivers the milk—forgetting for the moment that virtually no one delivers milk anymore and ignoring the possibility that this person may, in fact, be a woman. To non-native speakers, however, these relationships may not be as obvious as they seem. A "snowman," for example, is *not* a man who delivers snow but a figure made of snow. We'd be pretty unhappy if the garbage man delivered garbage and would be doubly distressed if he turned up not only carrying but also constructed from garbage. A doorman neither delivers nor removes doors, nor is he made of them.

Learners soon discover that English words may be combined in myriad ways to form new words, but the meanings of combined forms may be harder to work out than a native speaker assumes. In fact, English words are notorious for failing to mean what they should! Idioms, expressions whose meaning can't be worked out by examining their individual parts, have a special notoriety. Most second language learners attest that learning idiomatic expressions is a major challenge and one they sometimes despair of meeting. "Double-cross," for example, is one that gives learners trouble. Similarly, trying to work out the meaning of "hit the road" or "take a powder" can be frustrating, especially when learners believe they know the meaning of each individual word. They soon discover that knowing every possible meaning of each word in the phrase is of little value in making sense of the expression.

To work out the meanings of idioms, learners must either learn to use the context or, when this doesn't work, as it frequently doesn't, simply memorize the expression and its meaning. Either way, they're likely to make mistakes when they overgeneralize the use of an idiom or use it in an inappropriate context. For instance, the term "buck" is widely used for "dollar" in the United States and Canada. Its use, however, is restricted to certain situations. A salesclerk, for example, wouldn't respond to a customer's question about the price of an expensive garment by saying, "Six hundred bucks," at least not if she or he had any hope of closing the sale. The customer, however, might respond by saying, "Six hundred bucks is a lot to pay for a coat!" It's important for learners to master these distinctions if they are ever to master English completely.

## Cognates and False Friends

We've seen that English has been influenced by a number of other languages during its history. For this reason, many English words have close approximations in other languages. The French "boeuf," "porc," "chance" and "essence" are only a few of the words that have near equivalents in English. Similarly, the meanings of Spanish words such as "estructura" and "confusio" are pretty much the same as their English sound-alikes. This makes it tempting to believe that speakers of languages with many words that are similar to English are likely to find English easy to learn.

Unfortunately, however, this isn't the case. While languages that are closely related to English, such as French, have many cognates, in most languages with cognates there are at least as many false friends. False friends are English words that resemble words in the student's native language in sound or spelling but, in fact, have very different meanings.

Many years ago, when I was teaching Peruvian students in New Hampshire, a young woman recounted her disastrous experience in a pharmacy, where she requested a remedy for her condition, which she described as "constipado." The pharmacist promptly recommended a mild laxative, which she took. Needless to say, it had little effect on her real problem, a head cold. There are as many false friends in English and Spanish as there are in English and most Latin and Germanic languages. German and Dutch are especially renowned for being fickle.

SENTENCE STRUCTURE

Despite the fact that most of us rarely speak in complete sentences, we still consider the sentence to be the basic unit of expression. Certainly learning how words and morphemes combine to produce grammatical sentences is a central part of learning a new language. Sentence structure, or syntax, refers to the order in which words appear in sentences, as well as the elements that constitute the major components of sentences.

The importance of linear order is obvious; if we arbitrarily rearrange the words in an English sentence, the results may be disastrous. Imagine what would happen if a sports editor mixed up the normal subject-verb-object (SVO) order when writing the headline, "Orioles defeat Blue Jays," when, in fact, the Blue Jays had won the game. Fans would not be amused.

English is an SVO language, meaning that in most sentences with transitive verbs, the subject precedes and the object follows the verb. In addition, adjectives usually precede the nouns they modify, as in "the old, black house" or "a rundown garage."

Most learners quickly master these basics of word order, even though the word order of many of the world's languages is more flexible than English. Spanish, Italian and Chinese, for example, are primarily SVO languages, but all have more freedom in sequencing words than English. Word order that is considered poetic or quaint in English, such as, "Today came very late the letter carrier," is quite acceptable in Spanish as a way of emphasizing "letter carrier." Nevertheless, Spanish speakers have little difficulty grasping the fact that English word order is more rigid. Even Japanese students, accustomed to SVO word order, have relatively little difficulty with English word order. Nor do they have trouble with ordering smaller units, such as prepositions. In English, the preposition comes before a noun (that's what preposition means—before the position of a noun), but the comparable form in Japanese follows the noun.

Also essential to our comprehension and production of sentences is an understanding of how morphemes are organized into coherent groupings or units that are themselves organized into larger groupings or units within a sentence. These units include such basic sentence elements as noun phrases and verb phrases.

To read English accurately, it's necessary to understand constituent structure. For instance, consider the sentence: "Enthusiastic Toronto baseball fans relish the idea of another series of home games." A learner with limited vocabulary and little familiarity with the basic constituent structure of English—not to mention baseball!—might read this sentence several times without finding a verb. Alternatively, a learner might mistakenly assume that the subject noun phrase ends with "baseball" and the verb is "fans."

## Summary of Differences

I've attempted to paint in broad strokes the areas in which the differences between English and other languages can cause problems for learners of English. In their book, *Learner English*, Michael Swan and Bernard Smith describe in detail the language problems encountered by speakers of more than nineteen languages. The table on the following pages summarizes some of the more visible differences between English and Chinese, Vietnamese, Spanish and Japanese that may cause difficulty when speakers of these languages are learning English.

## Language Transfer

In describing some of the differences between other languages and English, I've probably given the impression that negative transfer, or interference, is a major obstacle to learning a second language. But is this true? If the similarity between the structure or vocabulary of the first and second languages played a significant role in language learning, then German and French speakers would be likely to have an easier time learning English than Russian or Arabic speakers. Following this line of reasoning, Chinese and Korean speakers would have the most difficulty because their languages aren't derived from the same Indo-European family as the others. My own experience—and that of my colleagues—doesn't support this view. There are certainly differences in the errors made

Common Differences between English and Four Other Languages

| English Feature | Chinese | Vietnamese | Spanish | Japanese |
|---|---|---|---|---|
| Vowel sounds | Fewer vowel sounds. No /æ/ or contrast between /i/ & /ɪ/ or /u/ & /ʊ/. | 11 vowel sounds plus diphthongs & triphthongs. | 5 pure vowel sounds & 5 diphthongs. No schwa. | 5 pairs of long-short vowels. Some voiceless vowels. |
| Consonant sounds | No /v/, /θ/, /ð/, /h/, /z/, /ǰ/, /č/, /š/ or non-nasal, word-final consonant. | No /f/, /θ/, /ð/, /z/, /s/, /ž/, /š/, /ǰ/. Initial /t/ is unaspirated. | /v/, /z/, /s/, /ž/, /ǰ/, /h/. | /l,r/ neutralized to flapped /r/, created by flapping the tongue quickly. No /θ/ or /ð/. |
| Consonant clusters | None initially or finally. | Some. No final "s" after a consonant. | Less frequent. Words don't begin with "s" plus another consonant. | None. |
| Other syllabic features | More stressed syllables. Monosyllabic structure. | More stressed syllables. Monsyllabic structure. | Strong devoicing of final consonants. | CV is dominant syllable structure. |

| English Feature | Chinese | Vietnamese | Spanish | Japanese |
|---|---|---|---|---|
| Prosodic features | Tonal. Little sentence intonation. | Tonal. Every syllable stressed. | Emphatic stress expressed by pitch rather than volume changes and falls on last syllable of sentence. | Some similar to English, but certain attitudes conveyed by intonation in English are conveyed by adverbials or other parts of speech. |
| Spelling & Pronunciation | Non-alphabetic. | Entirely phonetic. | Entirely phonetic. | Has both syllabic & non-phonological character systems. |
| Inflections | None. | None. | More highly inflected verb system. | Some inflections. Verbs not inflected for number or person. |
| False friends | None. | None. | Many. | Few. |

| English Feature | Chinese | Vietnamese | Spanish | Japanese |
|---|---|---|---|---|
| Word order | Primarily SVO & AN, but more flexible than English. | SVO & NA, fixed. | SVO & AN but more flexible than English. | SOV & AN. |
| Time relations | Time not related to verb tense. | Time not related to verb tense. | Time relations expressed by tense, but differs somewhat from English. | Time relations expressed by tense but differs somewhat from English. |
| Question formation | No auxiliaries or inverted word order. Question particle. Frequent use of tag questions. | No inverted word order. Question particle. | No fixed word order or auxiliaries. | No inverted word order. Question particle. |
| Other features | Same logogram can be verb or adjective. | No impersonal "it" as subject. Passive relatively rare. | Gender and number marked in nouns & adjectives. | No auxiliary verbs. No prepositions—comparable forms follow nouns. |

by speakers of different languages that may be attributed to the properties of their native language, but, overall, the capacity to develop a high level of proficiency in English is unaffected by the particular native language a learner knows.

Our earlier look at some of the strategies children use to learn English indicated that it's common for people to transfer rules from the native language to the new language. But, as we've seen in this chapter, the differences between languages means that this strategy sometimes leads to errors. For example, Chinese speakers tend to produce the voiceless equivalent of normally voiced English consonants, pronouncing "zoo" as "soo" or "live" as "life." This error is usually attributed to the fact that Chinese has no /z/ or /v/, so Chinese speakers substitute the closest sounds that do exist in Chinese. Similarly, it's often argued that French and German speakers have difficulty with the sounds made by "th" in English because their languages have no equivalent. This is a convenient assumption but, in the case of children, it may be faulty.

The source of errors may not always be obvious. During the 1980s, I conducted a series of studies with five-year-olds who were learning English as a second language in British Columbia. Because I'd observed that children in the first four or five years of school rarely had serious pronunciation problems, I was primarily interested in their learning of the sound system. Over the course of an entire school year, I recorded and analyzed a massive amount of the English language spoken by sixteen kindergarten children. One of the things I learned was that children made essentially the same pronunciation errors, whatever their native language. In other words, no matter which language they learned first, they mastered English sounds gradually, making the same kinds of substitutions and approximations for sounds they found difficult.

I found their learning of the sounds made by "th"—/θ/ as in "thin" and /ð/ as in "this"—particularly intriguing. At the beginning of the year, the children seemed quite able to produce these sounds. Gradually, however, they seemed to lose this ability and began to substitute a dentalized version of /t/ and /d/ by placing their tongues just behind the upper teeth instead of between the upper and lower teeth. Most children maintained this pronunciation only for a short time. Then they began to substitute /t/ and /d/ for the sounds made by "th," producing "tink" for "think" and "dis" for "this." This substitution continued for several months before a curious thing began to happen. Many of the children returned to the dentalized pronunciation for a few days or weeks before finally achieving the correct pronunciation. For the most part, once they mastered this, they maintained it, though some of them occasionally reverted to earlier incorrect pronunciations. This tended to happen at times when they were experiencing rapid growth in other areas of language, such as vocabulary or sentence structure.

Because I studied children from eight different language backgrounds and because I found their behavior so consistent, I've come to think differently about what causes errors. It seems to me, first, that much of what we think of as error is really only a phase in the developmental process. In other words, in the course of learning English, children make similar kinds of mistakes, no matter what their native language. Second, it seems likely that many of the articulation errors can be attributed as much to the nature of the language being learned as to the language they already know. What the children in my studies had in common, other than their age, was the fact that all were learning English. If these observations hold true, and my reading of the research literature suggests that they do, then we must think very carefully about correction. It is likely that it plays only a minimal role, if any at all, in helping young learners progress through the stages toward accurate pronunciation.

I realize, of course, that teachers may find it very difficult to adopt a hands-off approach to errors. It is helpful, though, if we can stop thinking of children's language as an inaccurate version of adult English and start thinking of it as a developing system in its own right. This requires a profound shift in the way we think about children's language; it means viewing it in positive terms, appreciating what the learner knows and is accomplishing. In this view, mismatches between children's pronunciation and adult pronunciation become evidence of what the child knows about the English sound system. When the pronunciation changes, we recognize that the change signals that the child has developed a new "rule" or understanding about the language. We must have faith that children will eventually recreate the adult system without our constantly pointing out their errors.

When audio-lingual methods were popular, special emphasis was placed on eradicating errors. The belief, consistent with the dominant learning theory of the time, was that learning a new language meant acquiring a new set of linguistic habits. Errors were to be prevented because their existence meant teachers would be spending time extinguishing bad habits rather than instilling good ones. Today, there is less emphasis on errors because researchers and teachers have come to understand that many errors are developmental, a natural part of interlanguage, the transitional stage in learning a new language when a changing system of rules governs a non-native learner's speech.

Nevertheless, it is useful for teachers to understand why speakers of certain languages routinely make certain errors when they speak English. Sometimes, by simply pointing out a difference between an English and a native language structure, by drawing learners' attention to the cause of an error, teachers go a long way toward eliminating the error.

## HELPING ESL CHILDREN
## WITH SPECIAL NEEDS

Earlier chapters indicated that children succeed in learning additional languages despite major differences in background, environment, and learning styles and strategies. The road to bilingualism is relatively smooth for them. For 2 to 3 per cent, however, the journey is rockier. Children who are born with or who acquire disorders that inhibit their ability to learn languages or communicate effectively face special challenges in second language classrooms.

I thought about titling this chapter "Learning a Language When You're the Underdog." I didn't, not because this title fails to capture the sense of what the chapter is about, but because it gives the impression that children with special needs are somehow deficient. In fact, while these children do have distinctive needs, what is deficient is usually our ability to meet these needs. Before we can do so, we must be able to identify what they are. When children's English proficiency is limited and we don't understand their first language, identifying needs that go beyond those associated with the task of learning a second language may not be easy.

### Communicative Disorders

A great many physical, emotional and cognitive conditions may impair children's language learning and, indeed, their learning in general. In these few pages, there isn't room to describe all the disabilities and disorders that may impede language and learning. Many are so rare that most teachers are unlikely to encounter them at all. Besides, many authors have already devoted fine articles and books to them, and there is no point in my even trying to duplicate their efforts. What I would like to do, though, is describe some of the more common communicative disorders teachers are likely to encounter.

Communicative disorders are those that result in speech that is so flawed that it interferes with children's ability to make themselves understood. Although the disorder itself may not inhibit learning, it may impede normal communication, a circumstance that may interfere with children's opportunities to use and learn language. Communication disorders fall into four broad categories related to voice production, fluency, articulation of particular sounds, and language processing.

VOICE PRODUCTION DISORDERS

At some time or other, a bad cold or sore throat has probably left most of us hoarse. Fortunately, this usually passes within a few days and our voice quality returns to normal. However, people whose voices always sound hoarse may be suffering from a voice disorder. Hoarseness, excessive breathiness or extreme nasality may all be considered voice disorders if they persist and if they appear to affect both a child's languages.

There are two basic kinds of voice disorder. The first result from an abnormality in the vibration of the vocal folds, or chords, during speech. These might cause hoarseness, especially apparent during the production of vowel sounds and consonants such as /l/, /r/, /m/ and /n/ or they might cause excessive breathiness.

The second is caused by an abnormality in the resonance of a sound. The human vocal tract consists of two large cavities, the oral cavity and the nasal cavity. In normal, rapid speech production, the velum, at the back of the oral cavity, rapidly opens and closes according to whether the sound produced is primarily oral—created in the mouth—or nasal—created in the nose. When the velum either doesn't close off the nasal cavity when it should or closes it off when it shouldn't, the result is a resonance disorder. For example, consider what normally happens when we articulate a word such as "cat." Because there is no nasal sound in the word, the velum closes off the nasal passage and the entire word is produced without any resonance in the nasal cavity. When we produce a word such as "man," however, there are two nasal sounds—/m/ and /n/. The nasal cavity is open when these sounds are produced and, because the vowel is tucked between them, it has a nasal quality as well. A person with a "leaky velum," one kind of voice disorder, produces excessively nasal-sounding language. Blockages in the nasal cavity itself may also produce a strange-sounding resonance.

While there are many causes of voice disorders, only about a third are anatomical or neurological. Some are physical, such as prolonged abuse of the vocal chords during screaming or singing, but these are likely to be temporary, requiring no intervention other than rest. Another cause is emotional stress, which may or may not be related to the second language learning experience.

In some instances, there is no real disorder at all. Rather, the learner may be applying certain "rules" of the native culture to voice production in the target culture. For instance, what sounds like excessive breathiness to us may be a normal or desirable trait in the speech of some cultures. If you are unsure, ask around to find out whether others have detected the trait in children from the same culture or telephone your community's immigrant-serving agency and ask to talk to someone from that culture. If these enquiries indicate that this isn't the problem and if it persists for more than a few weeks, interfering with communication or marking the child as different in a way that makes either you or the child uneasy, then the child should be referred to a speech or language specialist for evaluation. Be sure that you tell the professional everything you've learned about the child's language abilities and cultural background.

FLUENCY DISORDERS

Children who have fluency disorders have trouble speaking rapidly and continuously. The rate or rhythm of their speech, and sometimes both, may be abnormal. Stuttering, the best-known fluency disorder, is fairly easy to identify. In afflicted bilingual children, stuttering may affect either or both languages, and only rarely is there a physiological cause. Other fluency disorders include cluttering and long hesitations.

Children with a cluttering disorder produce a series of words very rapidly, then often pause before starting to speak again. Their speech is so rapid that the words may be unintelligible to most listeners.

Children afflicted with hesitation problems, on the other hand, pause often and for unnaturally long periods and may repeat themselves unnecessarily. Hesitation is a phenomenon that occurs frequently in the speech of normally developing children at around the age of three and then disappears. Induced by stress or trauma, it can occur on a temporary basis in speakers of any age.

Diagnosing communication disorders in bilingual children is not always easy. Children learning a new language may hesitate, make false starts and repeat themselves, making them difficult to understand. Some may develop a temporary stutter, probably because of the emotional stress they are experiencing in the new language and culture. Other ESL learners may adopt a strategy of speaking very rapidly to cover up gaps in their vocabulary or uncertainty about pronunciation. Although these may sound like fluency disorders, they aren't because they are temporary, induced by the situation.

Before deciding whether to refer a child with a suspected fluency disorder to a specialist, teachers should consider one further fact. Not all cultures take the same view of stuttering, hesitancy and other fluency problems as English speakers. In other words, what the teacher may view as a problem may not be considered one by the children's parents. So tread carefully and be patient, keeping in mind that the ultimate goal is fluent, proficient communication in English. If there is no explanation for the onset of the problem, if it significantly interferes with a child's ability to communicate, and if it persists for more than a few weeks, then make the referral.

Where most fluency disorders are concerned, the prognosis for improvement is excellent. This is one area in which practice is well ahead of theory in the sense that speech and language therapists understand far more about treatment than they do about causes.

Articulation disorders comprise a wide range of problems and may be among the most difficult to identify in bilingual children. Some articulation disorders involve difficulty in pronouncing a particular sound or class of sounds—sibilants, for instance—and have little effect on intelligibility. Others are far more serious and may result in total incomprehensibility. Fortunately, disorders of this magnitude are usually detected before a child reaches school age.

As we talk about articulation disorders, it's important to distinguish between deviance and delay. As children acquire their first language, they routinely simplify the adult sound system to one their immature cognitive and articulatory ability can manage. In doing so, they neutralize certain distinctions, making the same sound do double or triple duty. For example, most children produce the sounds /l/, /r/, and /w/ as /w/ for a time, meaning that words like "rise," "lies" and "wise" all sound the same. While they usually work out the distinction by the age of three or so, some don't produce all three sounds until they reach school age. Their production may be delayed, but it isn't necessarily deviant. Most children will eventually acquire the adult pronunciation of all the sounds of their language, including the problematic /l/, /r/, and /w/, without intervention.

Deviance refers to aspects of the child's phonological system that differ from those of other children of any age. How do we tell the difference between deviance and delay? First, consider the case of a child whose pronunciation is noticeably different from that of her peer group. There are two possible explanations. If the child's phonological system seems to be essentially the same as that of a younger child, then it isn't deviant but simply delayed. On the other hand, if her speech shows evidence of patterns that *never* appear in younger children, then her system is likely deviant. If phonological deviance is suspected, teachers should refer the child to a speech therapist or language pathologist who will be able to confirm whether there is a problem and recommend treatment, if necessary.

Bilingual children, of course, may present a diagnostic challenge. Because their pronunciation routinely deviates from that of native speakers, their articulation disorders may go unnoticed for a longer period than those of monolingual children. Conversely, there is a risk that an articulation disorder may be identified too quickly when, in fact, their pronunciation is the result of a normally developing interlanguage system.

Interlanguage refers to the language system used at an intermediate stage of comprehending and producing a second language. We might think of it as a short list of simple rules used by second language learners at a time when their exposure to and knowledge of the new language is limited. It's worth noting that these "rules" are the learners' own hypotheses about how the new language works. They are not the rules written down in books or provided by teachers.

At this time, their hypotheses about the new language may be influenced by what they know about their native language. Thus, the sounds they produce in English may be influenced by similar, but different, sounds in their own language, as we saw in an earlier chapter. They may produce forms that seem deviant but are, in fact, simply borrowed from their first language. Once again, we must do a little detective work if we are in doubt about whether a particular pronunciation is in fact deviant.

Not all differences in ESL learners' pronunciation can be attributed to the native language, however. In the previous chapter, I outlined the results of a study that indicated a strong similarity in the simplifications children make in the English sound system, no matter what their native language. The sixteen children in the study, who spoke several different first languages, followed the same sequence of development in learning the pronunciation of "th." This suggested that developmental sequences exist independent of the native language. They may occur either because the common language being learned is English or because there is a natural tendency in human learning to approximate the correct form gradually and systematically.

When teachers encounter a child who has difficulty producing certain sounds, whether the difference is attributable to transfer or other causes, my advice is to wait and see. If there is any change, even if it is not to the correct form, then there is likely no problem. If, in a few months, the aberrant pronunciation continues while the child's language grows in all other respects, it will be necessary to do a little sleuthing to find out whether other children with the same language background experience similar problems. If there is no evidence that they do, then a referral to a specialist is probably in order. As with all suspected disorders, look for a specialist who is accustomed to working in a multicultural setting and tell him or her everything you know about the child's background and language history.

LANGUAGE DISORDERS

So far, we've looked at communicative disorders that affect the intelligibility of speech. The fourth category of disorders may affect not only speech but also a wider range of language skills or abilities. Known as language disorders, they include a broad spectrum of dysfunctions that impair one or more of the skills involved in speech, listening comprehension, reading and writing. This impairment is a result of damage to the child's underlying language system, usually caused by a mental or physical affliction.

The disorders themselves vary in severity and in the language skill they affect. Those caused by specific damage to the brain are called aphasias. Aphasia refers to the loss of the ability to use or understand language, but excludes disabilities caused by physical ailments outside the brain, such as deafness or blindness. While there are many different kinds of aphasia, distinguished by the particular area of the brain that is damaged, they are usually classified into three types— receptive or sensory aphasia, expressive aphasia and global aphasia.

As the name suggests, receptive aphasia affects a child's ability to comprehend speech and, sometimes, to retrieve words from memory. Children with receptive aphasia may be extremely fluent and have no obvious articulation disorders. Their fluency, however, may be marked by repeated phrases, formulaic phrases or even meaningless sequences of words, produced in some cases because they don't comprehend and can't monitor their own speech.

Expressive or motor aphasia interferes, usually severely, with the ability to speak. Both articulation and fluency are affected, and children with this disorder speak very slowly, in short sentences and with many hesitations and disturbances to the individual sounds. Their intonation patterns are also atypical. Most expressive aphasics, however, have near-normal comprehension abilities.

Children with global aphasia exhibit some symptoms of both receptive and expressive aphasia. Their speech capacity is minimal and their comprehension is also poor. This is the most serious of the aphasias and, unfortunately, the prognosis for recovery or even significant improvement is poor. Diagnosis and treatment are beyond the expertise of classroom teachers and must be carried out by a trained professional. It's highly unlikely that a child with global aphasia would reach school without being diagnosed. However, in very rare cases, an aphasic child who has spent years in a refugee camp or traveling the world seeking refuge may have gone undiagnosed.

Some apparent language disorders may have more common causes. A child with some degree of hearing loss, for example, may experience problems with both comprehension and articulation. In fact, I always advise teachers who are worried about abnormal speech of any kind to have the child's hearing tested. Because between 6 and 7 per cent of the population suffers some degree of hearing impairment, we'll likely encounter the occasional child whose speech is affected by this problem, which is usually correctable. Similarly, some reading problems are the result of visual impairments, a possibility teachers should investigate if children have trouble reading fluently or recognizing words or letters.

## Semilingualism

In this chapter, I've touched briefly on four categories of communicative disorders found in both monolingual and bilingual children. I'd like to conclude with a note on a relatively rare language condition that afflicts only bilingual children. I emphasize that the condition is extremely rare—in fact, some researchers believe that it doesn't exist at all. While my own experience has convinced me that it does, it's worth noting that I've encountered only two cases in twenty-three years.

The term used to describe this condition is semilingualism. It's used in Europe, primarily in Scandinavia, to refer to bilingual children who have mastered neither of their languages well enough to succeed in school. The term is not widely used in North America for reasons I'll discuss later. For now, let's consider the children and the condition it describes.

Long ago, teachers and researchers noticed that children being educated in a second language are more likely to achieve success at school if their native language is the dominant language of the community. An English-speaking child learning French in an immersion class in Manitoba, then, is less "educationally at risk" than a Haitian child learning English in the same province. Researchers have also noted that some children seem to derive more benefit from their bilingualism than others and that older children being educated in a non-native setting are more successful than younger children.

As outlined in an earlier chapter, Canadian researchers Jim Cummins and Merrill Swain found that school success is more closely related to children's proficiency with cognitive academic language than it is to their interpersonal communication skills. They went on to hypothesize that second language learners need to attain a certain threshold level of proficiency in the new language before they can benefit from it as the language of instruction at school. Moreover, Jim Cummins asserted that the level of second language proficiency children achieve depends on the level of proficiency they have attained in their first language at the time extensive exposure to the second language begins.

These hypotheses—known as the threshold hypothesis and the interdependence hypothesis—were developed to account for the fact that ESL children who come to school with little or no cognitive academic proficiency in either of their languages are likely to be less successful than children who have acquired some cognitive academic proficiency in at least one. In extreme cases, children's basic interpersonal communication skills *and* their cognitive academic language proficiency may be poorly developed in both languages. These children are referred to as semilingual.

The two cases of semilingualism I've seen—as well as other suspected cases reported to me—have certain elements in common. My first encounter involved a little boy from the Philippines whom I met about ten years ago when I was conducting research in a grade one classroom. I spent two mornings a week in his school, dividing my time among two kindergarten classes and his grade one class. I first met Rusty, short for Restituto, during the first week of school when the teacher was assessing his English language proficiency. She had concluded, and I concurred, that Rusty needed ESL support and, in consultation with the school's ESL teacher, was in the process of deciding what form that help should take.

It wasn't uncommon for this process to take a few weeks. The teacher wanted to get to know Rusty, watch him interact with other children and assess informally whether he had particular language strengths or weaknesses that her initial assessment had missed. She had often found, for example, that children who did poorly on the initial formal assessment knew far more English than the test indicated, much of it learned very quickly in the company of English-speaking peers. In many cases, these children fared quite well when learning to read.

Rusty's vocabulary, however, remained extremely limited and the teacher observed that he was reluctant to engage with other children. She and the ESL teacher settled on a plan to keep Rusty in the grade one classroom most of the time but have him work for forty-five minutes three times a week with the ESL teacher and two other children his age. When the plan was explained to Rusty's father, however, Mr. L, as I shall call him, made it very clear that he wouldn't go along with it. He didn't believe that his son belonged in an ESL class.

Rusty had been in Canada since shortly after his first birthday and his parents had ensured that he learned only English. As Mr. L explained it, his own progress through school had been hampered by his limited English and his Tagalog accent. Determined to make Rusty's experience with schooling more positive, Mr. L and his wife had spoken only English to him since birth. Because Rusty hadn't learned Tagalog, they were confident that his English was as good as a native speaker's. If their son were labeled an ESL child, they would view it as a "disgrace."

In outlining Mr. L's concerns, I've failed to convey anything about his own English. It was heavily accented, although intelligible, and his sentences tended to be short and poorly formed. Although he was certainly able to communicate, he often searched for words, frequently settling on familiar ones that only approximated his intended meaning. He told us that he had come to school instead of Mrs. L because her English was not as good as his.

The teacher assured Mr. L that she would do her best to provide whatever help Rusty needed and would not place him in an ESL class against his parents' will. Mr. L left, apparently satisfied, and the teacher and I began to consider how to keep this promise and the effect doing so was likely to have on Rusty's success in school. We decided to establish an optional language enrichment program, available to all the children in the class. We were aware that we were taking a chance—because we planned to limit the groups to three or four children, it might be necessary to form as many as six or seven special enrichment groups. It was also possible that Mr. and Mrs. L might choose not to sign up Rusty.

We crossed our fingers and invited interested parents to a meeting where we planned to explain that the program might be especially important for children experiencing early problems with reading. We were lucky. Only five parents showed up to discuss the program and four requested that their children participate. Fortunately, Mr. L was one of them.

Over the course of the school year, it became obvious that the decision to provide additional language support for Rusty was the right one. Although he was a friendly and agreeable child, he tended to be quiet and stay aloof from the activities of the other children, even those of his own cultural group. It was obvious that he didn't understand much of their language, consistent with what his father had told us about the family's speaking only English at home. At the same time, he appeared to lack the English language skills to interact appropriately with the English speakers and made few attempts to join in their activities. While he did demonstrate some familiarity with a few popular children's books, he showed no interest in reading for himself and responded in one or two words, when he responded at all, to the teacher's questions about the stories.

Although I left the area at the end of that school year and had no further direct contact with Rusty, I stayed in touch with his teacher for several years afterward. Rusty found formal education a trying experience. For the first four years, he managed to pass from grade to grade but, according to his teachers in those years, his English language skills were never fully developed and he found schoolwork extremely difficult. When his family left the school district at the end of his fourth year, Rusty was reading at a grade two level.

Was Rusty semilingual? Certain elements of his story, particularly those that correspond with the facts of a clearer case I encountered a few years later, lead me to think so. This case, involving a child named Michael, is documented in my book *Language for All Our Children*. In both cases, the parents had themselves experienced problems in their adopted society and attributed these to their lack of English. Both considered it so important for their child to learn English that they effectively eradicated their native language from the home, working hard to communicate only in English. Neither set of parents was proficient in English and, in both cases, the language skills of the principal caregiver, the mother, were weaker than the father's.

While neither child spoke the parents' native language, both appeared to understand at least some. Rusty was the eldest child in his family and Michael the youngest, but Michael's sister moved out of the family home when he was about two-and-a-half-years-old. Both children had extreme language problems, Michael's being worse than Rusty's, yet the cognitive ability of both seemed to be normal.

While it seems that Michael and probably Rusty were semilingual, I'm reluctant to apply this label to either of them. My fear is that if this term comes into widespread use, it will be applied to children unfairly. Like many labels, it may be used to dump blame on the "victim." Teachers may assume that certain bilingual children don't do well in school because they didn't arrive there with the degree of language proficiency the school expects.

On the other hand, ignoring the needs of the few children who may truly have underdeveloped language skills in both their languages is also risky. As teachers, we need to take our time and use our professional judgment to determine the language ability and needs of each child. I know of no tests that can do this; teachers must simply observe children carefully in a variety of situations over a period of at least a few weeks.

We must also keep methodical records of children's language development. It's very easy to lose sight of children's progress when we see and hear "flawed" language on a daily basis. When I was studying Michael, I remember thinking at the end of the school year that he'd made little, if any, progress because his speech was still distorted and woefully limited in comparison with his peers. But when I went back to the recordings I'd made early in the year, I realized how mistaken I was. Measured against this standard, the improvement in his speech was significant.

We must also forget about labeling. What we call a problem will do nothing to improve matters for the children—and, in fact, may do damage. Finally, we must provide these children with opportunities for growth by creating the richest language environment we can.

If we think about it, the preceding advice may be appropriate for helping children suspected of having any of the problems discussed in this chapter and, indeed, all children. There is almost never a risk in adopting a wait-and-see attitude, good record-keeping is part of being an effective teacher, labeling seldom serves any purpose, and all children benefit from being in classrooms where talk and reading and writing—their language—is valued and encouraged to flourish.

. . . . . . . . . . . . . . .

# PLANNING PROGRAMS

We've seen that children become bilingual under a variety of circumstances. We've also seen that there are often marked differences between children's language-learning experiences at home and at school and in the way students approach the business of learning. As teachers, our responsibility is to provide the most effective learning experience possible for each of the children we encounter. Of course, the question then becomes, How? Do we plan for each child individually? Or is it possible to construct programs that are appropriate for most children and flexible enough to adapt for all?

A number of program alternatives have been used with school-aged children. Mary Ashworth described many of them in *The First Step on the Longer Path*. While this was certainly not her intent, the risk in providing a list of options is that people sometimes fail to look beyond these for other, more creative—and possibly more appropriate—alternatives.

The title of this chapter may suggest that ESL programs come already packaged, ready for unwrapping and delivery. In a way, this is true, for schools have successfully used a number of programs with ESL learners over the past few decades. While these sometimes meet the needs of particular ESL classes or individuals, they often require modification. Before any programming decision can be made, teachers must have certain kinds of information about students. This chapter reviews briefly the program alternatives Mary Ashworth described, then goes on to consider factors we must take into account when choosing and modifying any of them.

## ESL Programs

Mary Ashworth identified four basic program categories—self-contained programs, withdrawal programs, transitional programs and mainstreaming—commonly used with ESL students, as well as variations of each.

In self-contained programs, beginning students study English in the same classroom for all or a large part of the school day. Students in withdrawal programs have enough English to participate successfully in at least some regular classroom activities, but are withdrawn to work with an ESL teacher for specified periods during the day. Transitional, or bridging, programs help students make the transition between ESL and regular classrooms and include options such as subject matter classes with simplified language, academic booster classes and vocational pre-employment classes. ESL students who are mainstreamed are placed in the mainstream class but provided with some language support. Immersion qualifies as a mainstream option, but English immersion is relatively rare in English-speaking countries.

The table on the following pages summarizes the features of each program as well as variations that may occur within each category.

## Selecting Programs

With four broad programming options and several alternatives within each to choose from, how do we select an appropriate program for an individual student or group? Or would an entirely different kind of program be more effective?

The following are some of the questions I've been asked over the years, as well as some that should have been asked. For the most part, they deal with the problems teachers face in reconciling the facts about children's acquisition of a second language with certain realities of the educational system.

*If children successfully learn languages under so many different conditions, why must we be so concerned with programs? At home, children learn one or more languages without being taught. There are also many stories of children picking up language without*

Program Options

| Program Type | Levels | English Proficiency | Recommended Class Size | Advantages | Limitations |
|---|---|---|---|---|---|
| **Self-Contained** | | | | | |
| Full-day reception | Kindergarten through high school | Beginner may require a full year. Intermediate may need only a few weeks or months. | 10-15 depending on age and proficiency. | Intensive language training. Teacher understands linguistic, cultural & emotional needs. | Limited exposure to English-speaking peers. Time lost from content courses. Teacher must be very flexible. |
| Half-day reception | Kindergarten through high school | Beginner integrated into classes with low language demand. Intermediate integrated into wider range of courses. | 10-15 | Intensive language training. Some individualization possible. Teacher understands linguistic, cultural & emotional needs. | |

| Program Type | Levels | English Proficiency | Recommended Class Size | Advantages | Limitations |
|---|---|---|---|---|---|
| Bilingual | Kindergarten through high school | All | 15-20 if similar in age & ability, otherwise 10-15 | Teacher understands both languages & cultures. Children become literate in both languages. Both languages valued & supported. Meaning easy to convey. | Students may neglect English language learning. May become "ghettoized." |
| **Withdrawal** | | | | | |
| English language center | Kindergarten through high school | Intermediate to advanced | Individuals or groups of 2-5 | Can be reception class. Individualization possible. Easy to consult with other teachers. | Not adequate for beginners, especially those under 8 & over 12. |

| Program Type | Levels | English Proficiency | Recommended Class Size | Advantages | Limitations |
|---|---|---|---|---|---|
| Itinerant teacher | Kindergarten through high school | Intermediate to advanced | Individuals or groups of 2-5 | Relatively inexpensive. Effective if teacher cooperates with classroom teacher. | Time lost to teacher travel. Difficult to organize coherent programs & consult with classroom teacher. |
| Tutorial | Kindergarten through age 13 or 14 | Intermediate to advanced | | | |

### Transition

| Program Type | Levels | English Proficiency | Recommended Class Size | Advantages | Limitations |
|---|---|---|---|---|---|
| Transitional subject-matter classes | Age 14 through end of high school | Intermediate to advanced | Up to 20-22 | Content parallels regular course material. Simplified language. Opportunity for team teaching. | If credit not given, student may be short of graduation requirements. ESL teacher may not know content. |

| Program Type | Levels | English Proficiency | Recommended Class Size | Advantages | Limitations |
| --- | --- | --- | --- | --- | --- |
| Vocational pre-employment | Age 15 through adult | Intermediate to advanced | 10-20 | Very practical for students uninterested in further academic education. | May become "dumping ground." Teacher must resist tendency to specialize language training. |
| Academic booster | Kindergarten through high school | All | 10-12 | Builds basic skills of students whose education has been disrupted. | Students may be unfairly labeled slow or disabled. |
| Special education | Kindergarten through high school | Children with learning disabilities only | Individualized | Good for children with cognitive, emotional or social problems. | Tendency to enroll children on basis of low language proficiency. |
| Preschool | Pre-kindergarten | Beginner to advanced | 10-15 | Headstart before entering kindergarten. | "Formal" language teaching can do harm. |

| Program Type | Levels | English Proficiency | Recommended Class Size | Advantages | Limitations |
|---|---|---|---|---|---|
| **Mainstreaming** | | | | | |
| Mainstream support | Age 9-17 | Beginner to advanced | Up to 50% of regular class with extensive support | Many English-speaking peers. Content & language learning integrated. | If children enter mainstream too early or without adequate support, may lose motivation and fall behind in language and content learning. Some require more language help. |
| Informal immersion or submersion | Kindergarten through high school | Advanced | Less than 10% of total class | Rapid increase in vocabulary & other language skills. | Fear of failure. Students may fall behind if language skills inadequate when they join class. |

*instruction. Won't they pick up English naturally if they're simply exposed to it?*

While it's true that children learn language at home under a variety of conditions that might be described as normal, conditions at school are anything but. Sitting at a desk for five hours a day listening to a teacher talking in an unknown language about an unfamiliar subject is not, by anyone's standard, normal for any child. There are fundamental differences between children's home and school language, and we must take these differences into account in planning an optimal environment for children's language learning.

A common misconception about language acquisition is that children require only exposure. While it's certainly true that exposure is necessary, it isn't the only thing required. A second misconception about language learning that operates alongside this often leads school administrators to ignore ESL children. This misconception concerns the nature of immersion programs in which the entire curriculum is taught in the new language rather than the native tongue. The best-known of these is in Canada where English-speaking children may choose an immersion program in which all subjects are taught in French.

To the uninformed, immersion is the same as submersion. They assume that placing ESL children in mainstream classrooms with no special support is the same as placing an English-speaking child in a French immersion classroom. Nothing could be farther from the truth. In the first place, immersion teachers speak both English and French so they can understand the children's English questions and responses. They are also very highly trained in making both the language and the content comprehensible.

On the other hand, non-English speakers left to fend for themselves in a classroom with native English speakers have neither a teacher nor, in many cases, other students who speak their language to turn to for help. As a method of language teaching, this is both inefficient and usually ineffective.

Just as children pick up colds and measles from exposure alone, they will also pick up some language. The problem is that it might not be the language they need to succeed in school. Remember that the language of the school is a different register from that of the home, television or playground.

School language is largely decontextualized, formal, abstract, logical and expository. The informal language of the home is, in contrast, context-bound, sequential and intuitive. It is the very fact that it is connected to real objects in real time that makes learning it seem so effortless. Language that has a real purpose and readily discernible meaning is easier to learn than that which has neither. This means that, in planning effective language environments for children, we must make the language accessible. To borrow Stephen Krashen's terminology, we must provide "comprehensible input."

*We've seen that children acquire second or third languages in much the same way as they learn registers of their native language. How should this fact inform our decision-making?*

Research tells us that the younger children are, (i.e., the closer they are to the experience of learning their first language), the more likely they are to adopt first-language learning strategies in learning a new language. One of these strategies is to consider all languages as variations of a single language, their language.

This being the case, we should be mindful of the circumstances under which children acquire their first language and plan accordingly. This means that we must consider the wide variety of functions language has in the life of a young child and make sure that whatever program we plan provides ample opportunity to develop all of them. It also means that we must keep in mind the circumstances under which children acquire their first language—as a means of communicating with others and learning about the world around them. Language and learning go hand in hand in the preschool years, and this relationship should continue throughout the school years.

For young children, then, we would choose programs that maximize contact with native-speaking peers and provide maximal simultaneous exposure to both language and the content areas. If we examine the table, we can see that this may require some modification to meet the needs of individual children, but mainstreaming with support is probably the best option in the early primary years.

*If there is, indeed, something special about the sound system of languages, does this mean that we should do something special about teaching the English system?*

No, quite the opposite is true. Children seem to give the sound system some kind of special status. Thinking about how the babbling of infants often sounds like they are talking long before they're able to articulate any real words, we can understand that sound is a special feature of language. When we also consider that young bilingual children mix the sound systems of their two languages less often than any other feature, we can further understand that they will master the sound system without any special intervention on the part of teachers or other adults.

There is evidence, however, that this special status may be lost as children grow older. Sometime around the age of puberty, most young people begin to have more difficulty with pronunciation, and the sounds of their native language may intrude on their speech in English. For adolescent learners, then, planning may need to include specialized components dealing with the discrimination of sounds that are either new to the student or found in different environments in English. The sounds made by "th" are, for example, relatively rare among the languages of the world, accounting for the fact that many Chinese, German and French speakers have trouble with "this," "that," "these" and other words containing "th." In planning programs for adolescents, we might need to include opportunities for specialized pronunciation practice.

*If children are truly capable of acquiring two languages simultaneously without detriment to either, shouldn't we be providing bilingual programs for all children?*

In an ideal world, this would certainly be the case. Children would have the opportunity to acquire the content of the entire school curriculum and become proficient in two languages at the same time.

Unfortunately, however, the real world of education is far from ideal. In the first place, most teachers find that the ESL children in their classes represent two, three, or as many as eight or nine different language groups. I once taught a kindergarten class in which fifteen different languages were represented among twenty children! It would be a rare school district that could afford to organize bilingual programs and hire bilingual teachers for all these languages. Even if they could afford it, it's highly unlikely that they could find enough professionally qualified teachers because even teacher education programs that do active recruiting attract relatively few bilingual teachers.

In the second place, if a school is truly bilingual, then it isn't only the minority language speakers who are required to learn another language. English speakers, too, must learn a second language. This has been tried at some schools in the United States with large enough populations of, for example, Spanish speakers to make it worthwhile. The results, however, have been mixed. By and large, the native Spanish speakers tend to be more successful at acquiring English than the English speakers are at acquiring Spanish.

Where other bilingual programs exist, they tend to be less ambitious. Two types are commonly used—maintenance and transitional. The principal goal of maintenance programs is to protect the child's native language while introducing the language of the school. Maintenance bilingualism is not popular in the United States, but has been used with some success in the United Kingdom and Canada. Because of its official policy of multiculturalism, Canada has initiated a number of bilingual maintenance programs in languages including German, Ukrainian, Hebrew, French, Spanish, Italian and Cree. The central difference between these and full bilingual programs is that the goals of maintenance programs don't include achieving academic proficiency in the native language, though some include achieving literacy. Rather, they focus on encouraging children to maintain communicative competence in their first language.

The principal goal of transitional bilingual programs is the gradual introduction of the second language in a school setting. Virginia Collier's findings, reported in an earlier chapter, about the relative difficulty experienced by five- and six-year-olds indicate that this is an effective option where feasible. In transitional bilingual programs, the home language is used throughout the first few years of school and the dominant language is introduced later.

Transitional programs are not widely used in North America, but neither are they entirely unknown. Canada has transitional programs in place for Chinese, Ukrainian, German,

Hebrew, Italian and some other languages. Public documents show that the United States has government-sponsored programs for fifty or more languages. Transitional bilingualism is more widely adopted in other parts of the world, especially in countries, such as India, that have a large number of indigenous languages. Unfortunately, these programs are plagued by many of the same problems that face full bilingual programs—the expense and difficulty of recruiting qualified bilingual teachers.

*How can information about first language acquisition be incorporated into our planning for second language learners?*

Very easily. In fact, at least two perspectives on language teaching are consistent with what we know about first language learning. The first comes from first language teaching and is called whole language. The second comes from second language teaching and is called communicative language teaching. The two approaches are similar in their underlying beliefs, and we can borrow from both with a high degree of confidence that we are creating a lively and fruitful environment for ESL learners.

Although whole language may be the most visible educational trend of the past two decades, even teachers who profess to be practitioners don't necessarily agree on what it entails. Indeed, even so-called experts disagree about the precise characteristics of this approach. Most would agree, however, that the definition Victor Froese offers in his book, *Whole-Language: Practice and Theory,* is representative: "We define whole language as a child-centered, literature-based approach to language teaching that immerses students in real communication situations whenever possible."

This definition tells us that whole language is an approach that can guide our teaching of ESL children. First, it is child-centered, meaning that children's previous experience of language and learning are valued and built upon in the school setting rather than discarded. It also means that our programming must include ample room for evaluating and meeting individual needs, a reason for keeping ESL classes small.

Second, whole language is literature-based and, especially for young children, this has important implications for second language teaching. We've already seen that there is a discrepancy between the language children learn at home and the language they encounter in school. A very good way of bridging this gap is through children's literature. Not only is it of high interest and thus motivating for children, but it is also an important introduction to the language and to the purposes and pleasures of books. We must also remember that the ability to read well is a highly significant predictor of success at school and that the children who are most successful in learning to read are those who are read to.

Third, whole language immerses children in real communication situations, thus emulating language-learning experiences at home. Real communication is essential to language learning; a learner, even a highly motivated one, can progress only so far under artificial or contrived conditions. Besides, the need and the desire to communicate under actual conditions is intrinsically motivating.

Before moving on to the notion of communicative language teaching, I'd like to add a further note about whole language. As I write this, whole language is under increasing attack in the popular press. Some writers blame the so-called literacy crisis in North America on the adoption of the whole language approach in schools and call for a return to traditional phonics instruction. Teachers may be uneasy about extending a practice that is under attack into the second language program.

I'd like to reassure you, however, that only when the tenets of whole language are carried to the extreme do they put any learner at risk. If a teacher were to refuse outright to deal with English spelling or fail to respond to a child's enquiry about the relationship between sounds and letters or use whole language as an excuse not to teach required subjects in the curriculum, these would be extreme practices. They would be unfair and probably detrimental to children's learning.

Teachers who understand whole language also understand the importance of balance. True practitioners of whole language, because their attention is focused on the needs of individual children, do whatever is necessary to facilitate their language development. If, for some children, this includes a little traditional phonics instruction, then so be it.

Communicative language teaching, an approach to second language teaching that is consistent with the realities of first language learning, has certain parallels with whole language. Many books have been written and curricula designed around the tenets of communicative language teaching. Like whole language, it has many definitions and, again like whole language, most of these have certain common characteristics. The most important of these is the goal of helping learners develop communicative competence, or the ability to use the language appropriately in a variety of real situations.

Communicative language teaching emphasizes the processes of communication, such as using language to perform different kinds of tasks, get information or interact socially. Thus, it stresses the functions the second language must serve for the learner rather than simply the vocabulary and structure of the language. It recognizes that a second language, like the first, serves more than one function in a learner's life, but it goes beyond simply supplying the appropriate language by teaching appropriate language within the context of actual use when possible and providing realistic practice when not. In this respect, it is similar to the whole language approach.

Communicative language teaching is also similar to whole language in that it is learner-centered. In practice, this means that teachers or curriculum planners analyze the language needs of learners before attempting to plan their program of study. By centering on learners and focusing on real communication, the communicative approach provides students with an experience that is similar to their first language learning experience.

Once again, however, I must sound a warning. Communicative approaches are based on solid principles of language acquisition. Nevertheless, if the needs of the learner are ignored in favor of adhering rigidly to this or, indeed, any other method, then it will not succeed. Indeed, in these situations, I might argue that it is being used to abuse.

My experience in China provides an example of this. In a project I worked on there, a Canadian team was working with a Chinese team to write a curriculum for English majors in their first two years of study. Following the pedagogical bias and practice of our own culture at the time, we naturally pushed for a communicative curriculum. We introduced various models and samples and carefully explained the process.

The Chinese teachers listened carefully and then produced a copy of an examination students were required to write at the end of their first year. "Using your curriculum and methods, can you guarantee that our students will be able to pass this examination?" they asked. Because the test was long, very traditional and grammar-based, we could not make this guarantee. It didn't matter what we thought of the examination; it was a reality in the students' lives and we couldn't ignore it. The curriculum we eventually helped to write reflected this reality, even though it meant compromising the principles of the communicative approach.

*How do whole language and the communicative approach fit into existing program options?*

In theory, none of the programming options is incompatible with either whole language or the communicative approach. Just as it's possible to teach a reception class using a traditional audio-lingual or even a grammar translation approach (something I hope nobody would do, at least in elementary school), it's equally easy to plan around a communicative method. Certainly, communicative language teaching is the method of choice in many self-contained programs around the world and whole language is the preferred teaching method in many of the North American classrooms where ESL students will enter the mainstream.

While there is no necessary correspondence between program design and teaching approach, certain program options are more effectively realized using certain teaching methods. A pre-vocational program, for instance, would make little sense if it were taught using a grammar-translation approach. For such a program to be effective, content and language must be linked in ways that make both easy to learn, and this is accomplished with an approach that organizes its curriculum around content, as opposed to language forms, and provides opportunities for realistic and appropriate language practice. Bernie Mohan outlines a method like this in his book, *Language and Content.*

*The statistics on teacher talk quoted earlier are alarming to think about for any class, but do they have any special implications for second language learners?*

Yes, they have very profound implications. While it takes more than exposure to a language to learn it, exposure to comprehensible input is necessary. So is the opportunity to interact with native speakers and use the language for a variety of functions.

Consider the kind of exposure children get under the classroom conditions described by Claire Staab and outlined earlier in this book. Roughly half the time, they listen to the teacher lecture, probably understanding very little of what they hear. The rest of the time, they are either silent or listening to the teacher give directions, meaning that they are exposed mainly to the informing and directive functions of language and have almost no opportunity to explore any other function. Without opportunity for meaningful interaction in the language they are supposed to be learning, ESL children will become bored and frustrated.

This scenario would seem to argue against mainstreaming, as it should if no special support for ESL children is provided under this option. It's pointless for ESL children to sit in such a linguistically barren environment. They must be surrounded by a variety of language and have ample opportunity to use their developing English to create real meanings for real people. It all comes down to making the language experience of the school more closely parallel to the experience of the home, especially for younger learners.

*All right, this seems reasonable. But how do we do it? As teachers, we're responsible not only for teaching these children English but also for teaching them the subject matter outlined in the curriculum, a duality that isn't characteristic of home language.*

This is true, although I would still argue that we can borrow much from both whole language and the pedagogy of immersion. Children who enroll in immersion programs typically spend the entire first three years of schooling in the second language. These children don't know this language before they enter school, yet the Canadian experience indicates that English-speaking children in immersion classes are able to keep up with their monolingual peers—either French or English—in all school subjects.

While it's true that children in immersion classes tend to be from the more advantaged socioeconomic strata, it is also true that their accomplishment is remarkable. In large part, this is because methods of teaching in immersion are well-defined and developed and the teachers are well-trained in teaching the elementary school curriculum in a language that is unknown to the children.

Immersion is characterized by the exclusive use of the second language, usually French in North America. Because the children speak only English when they enter, teachers must be bilingual. They respond to the children in French, encouraging them to start using French themselves. Children who begin immersion in kindergarten usually start English language arts by their fourth or fifth year of school and the amount of English used in the classroom gradually increases until the proportion is approximately 60 per cent English and 40 per cent French.

For children to learn the subject matter and acquire the new language simultaneously, teachers must work very hard to make sure the input is comprehensible. Typically, they use a great many visual aids and make learning experiences as concrete as possible. Rather than talking about fractions using "concrete" examples, such as, "If I have one orange and three children want a piece of it...," teachers use the real object, divide it up, label the parts and provide the language for talking about fractions in the process.

The first children in the Canadian immersion experiment have now completed university. As might be expected, they have been extensively studied. Although the results are positive on the whole, it's clear that immersion doesn't create full bilingualism. Most researchers report that even after twelve years in immersion classes, anglophone children are still a long way from native proficiency. They have acquired impressive academic or "school" competence but less social language proficiency in French than they need to claim bilingual status. On the other hand, most researchers also agree that French immersion doesn't adversely affect the children's proficiency in English. Even though the English proficiency of some children may lag slightly behind that of their peers in their third and fourth year of school, they tend to catch up by the sixth and seventh year.

I'm not suggesting that immersion methods be adopted in ESL classrooms without modification. There are very significant differences between many ESL children and the advantaged anglophone children who typically populate immersion classes. Not the least among these is the support for the children's native language that exists outside the classroom, a luxury ESL children seldom have. Nevertheless, the immersion experience has taught us that it is possible for children to acquire language and learn content simultaneously and it would be foolish not to borrow methods that are appropriate for ESL children.

In particular, we should be thinking about how to make the regular classroom more like the immersion classroom—more "user friendly" for ESL children. No single program is right for all children, of course. But if we acknowledge the importance of basic interpersonal communication skills in developing academic or school language proficiency, then we begin to see how important peer interaction is for children. This means that whatever program we plan must provide plenty of opportunities for ESL children to interact with English-speaking children their own age.

There are many ways of doing this. Selective withdrawal programs that remove ESL children from the regular classroom for only limited periods give them both specialized ESL assistance and the chance to interact with their peers. Virginia Collier's study seems to suggest that for very young children, it's especially important to develop strong interpersonal language skills as a basis on which to build school language, indicating that ESL-supported mainstreaming is the best option. In other words, children should be allowed to remain in the regular classroom as much as possible while additional language support is provided, either within the classroom or in a limited withdrawal program.

For older learners, early mainstreaming is also desirable—but for different reasons. If they are isolated in ESL classes too long, the risk is that they will fall behind in demanding content areas. These students have more to learn than younger children—more language and more content. It is therefore essential that programs achieve the right balance between providing adequate language training and sufficient content. Bridge or transition classes help achieve this balance because they're designed either to teach content using simplified language or to teach the language by providing comprehensible content.

*Is there a good test I can use for placement purposes?*

Probably, but before testing any child, we should clearly understanding the following:

— Why we're testing the child; i.e., what the test will tell us about the child.
— What, if anything, the score will mean.
— What difference the score will make to our educational plans for the child.
— Whether the test will tell us things we don't already know or can't find out some other way.

Many seasoned ESL teachers have learned to trust their own assessment of learners' proficiency ahead of test scores. There is good reason for this. An educated adult speaker of English knows roughly 250,000 words. These can be combined into an infinite number of sentences appropriate for use in an endless variety of situations. The task facing ESL speakers is to learn the language well enough to deal with all the situations likely to come up in their lives.

From all possible words, structures and situations, test-writers select a limited number to measure learners' capabilities. A typical grammar test, for example, includes fifty questions with no more than 400 different words and perhaps as many as twenty different structures. A learner who answers half the questions correctly is considered halfway to native-like proficiency, but this judgment assumes that the items on the test represent an accurate sample of the students' knowledge base. In fact, students almost certainly know a lot of language that is never tested, language that the teacher has heard because he has spent more time talking to them in a variety of situations over a period of time that is certainly longer than the testing time.

Unless a test has clearly defined guidelines for interpreting the scores for placement and planning purposes, there is no point in giving it. The CanTEST is such a test for adult learners, but a version hasn't been written for school-aged children. Many elementary schools in Canada depend on a teacher's informal oral interview with children. There is little danger in this, after all. If the teacher misjudges the child's proficiency, she can move him or her to another class or make adjustments to the curriculum content.

*It appears that children's native language plays a role in determining some of the kinds of errors they're likely to make in learning English. In large school districts where there are language groups of significant size, wouldn't it make sense to place children in classes according to their native language so that teachers can work on the specific problems encountered by each group?*

While there might be some slight, temporary benefit to grouping children according to native language, I see more disadvantages than advantages in this—for both children and teachers. In the first place, interference from the native language is only one of the reasons for errors. Children learning English make remarkably similar errors no matter what their first language. This fact alone suggests that we should realign our thinking about errors, trying to think of them as marking stages of development or growth in the new language rather than as mistakes that must be eradicated. It would be a mistake to plan our programs on the basis of predicted errors.

In the second place, many other factors are more important in grouping children than native language. For example, it would make little sense to put a six-year-old with intermediate English language skills into a group of eleven- and twelve-year-olds simply because they all happen to speak Spanish. Age and level of proficiency are at least as important as native language in deciding how to organize ESL classes.

Third, grouping children on the basis of native language runs the real risk of creating educational ghettos. In every culture I've encountered, biases exist about other cultural and linguistic groups. It would be a grave error for teachers to bolster those biases, even inadvertently, by separating children according to ethnic background. Finally, ESL children need to be in the company of and have opportunities to play with and talk to children their own age whose first language is English. I oppose any grouping strategy that reduces these opportunities.

*Can one teacher or one program really accommodate all the different learning styles and strategies we read about earlier?*

Yes. Because children have always brought different learning styles to the classroom and used different strategies to learn when they got there, teachers have been doing just this for many, many years. Of course, cultural patterns or previous educational experience may be an additional factor influencing the styles and strategies of bilingual children. I see no reason, however, that these can't be accommodated. Remember, ESL children's styles and strategies won't differ greatly from those encountered in monolingual children.

*When strategy training was discussed earlier, retraining language style wasn't mentioned. Because some learning styles seem to be better-suited to school success than others, shouldn't we consider trying to retrain learning styles as we plan our curriculum and programs?*

No. I've always found it puzzling that professional educators, who certainly have the power to change the way they conduct the business of educating children, expend so much collective energy trying to find ways to change the children. Ostensibly, these changes are necessary to make children more compatible with the methods of the school. We seem to have a tendency to "blame the victim," to assert that children fail in school because they weren't adequately prepared at home or because they have difficult family lives. But surely we've got it backwards. Shouldn't the onus be on us to change schools to make them more hospitable places in which all children's learning styles can flourish?

As outlined earlier, learning styles are generally considered to be inherent, although it's likely that they're culturally influenced to some degree. This suggests very clearly that we should not try to tamper with them beyond, possibly, identifying them and providing the kind of learning experience that works best for each child.

*Is it really feasible to mainstream children with special needs when a class may already include a mixture of first and second language learners, the latter with varying levels of proficiency?*

I must confess that I suffer periodic doubts about mainstreaming children, whether monolingual or bilingual, with extreme disabilities. I'm also aware that saying so at this time is to express a politically unacceptable position. I think we must be very courageous on this issue and ask ourselves a very simple question—what's best for the child? Unfortunately, this question is much more easily asked than answered.

Last year, I visited a junior high school in which a 14-year-old boy from Ethiopia had just enrolled. The boy's teachers were very worried about their ability to provide for his educational needs because, in addition to knowing no English, he was blind and had a slight hearing loss.

I remember thinking that mainstreaming is an idea that works most of the time, but surely when a child is special in so many ways, unique arrangements must be made. Perhaps this boy's situation pushed the notion of mainstreaming to its limit. Not that it mattered. Mainstreaming is the official policy in my province and, if the boy's parents wanted him to attend this school, the school had no choice but to accept him. I talked to his teachers for a long time and, together, we came up with a number of strategies for meeting his needs. I must admit, however, that no one was very optimistic about his future.

As it turned out, we were wrong. I recently met a teacher from the school who told me that he is doing outstandingly. His oral language skills are excellent and he's learned to read English by braille. His marks in all subjects are well above passing and he seems contented in the school despite the fact that he's the only student with his particular language background. He has accomplished all this in mainstream classrooms. But, of course, it has not been his accomplishment alone. Countless hours of teachers' time—planning, teaching, helping and counseling—went into this success story.

This brings me to the most troubling aspect of mainstreaming students with extreme disabilities. The workload for their teachers, already burdened with responsibilities that go beyond the normal demands of what used to be considered teaching, is so greatly increased that they risk burnout. Burnout is a problem for us all because we can't afford to lose good teachers, and it's the good teachers who tend to be the ones who give so much to make broad mainstreaming work. The solution, I think, is to provide them with support—relief from non-teaching duties and smaller classes might be a start.

*Students in our school must write government-sponsored standardized tests at designated points in their school career, no matter how little English they know. The scores of ESL children with very limited*

*English are very low, a fact that is discouraging for them. How can we best prepare them for this particular reality of formal education?*

This is one of the many problems of evaluation and assessment faced by ESL teachers—and students—everywhere. Any form of standardized test is unfair to minority students. We must wonder why authorities continue to insist that all children write these examinations, whether or not they speak English and whether or not their education has been badly disrupted.

Their results are meaningless and may, in fact, skew the scores for an entire school or district. One of the ESL teacher's roles as advocate must be to lobby actively against this requirement. For the sake of this discussion, however, we'll accept that the tests must be given and concentrate on how best to prepare students to write them.

The very best preparation is literacy. Anything we can do in school to help ESL children develop their reading and writing skills and acquire the cultural knowledge required to be successful on these tests will improve their performance. It will probably help to spend a little time teaching test-taking skills—how to make a sensible guess on a multiple-choice test, avoiding leaving answers blank, etc. But without doubt, the best preparation is to help them acquire as much English as possible as soon as possible.

*What are some of the other factors schools should consider when planning programs for ESL learners?*

Principals and teachers want to provide the best education possible for all the children in their care. In addition to the questions raised here, a number of other issues should be considered.

The first is whether the program option under consideration limits or constrains the learner in any way. Sometimes, our best intentions actually interfere with children's inclination or ability to learn. For example, I recently visited an elementary school in Nova Scotia that had elected to institute a withdrawal program for kindergarten, grade one and grade two ESL children. The children were sent to the ESL teacher for 1½ hours each day. The teachers reasoned that the times the ESL children were out of the class should be worked around the "most important" subjects—language arts and math—so the children missed art one day, music the next, physical education on another, and so on.

After a few weeks, two of the children in grade one started refusing to go to the ESL class. At first, the teachers believed that they didn't like the ESL teacher or what she did with them or that they found the additional language work too great a strain. They were surprised to find out, however, that the children simply objected to missing parts of the day that they enjoyed. They saw other children getting out materials and preparing work, witnessed their excitement and pride at displaying their finished artwork and resented being denied the same opportunity.

From talking to a bilingual counselor, the classroom teacher learned that one of the children, a Chinese girl, had a special gift for drawing and deeply resented missing art even for one day. In this instance, the program plans limited the child's willingness and ability to benefit from the class.

Teachers must also think about whether the school can effectively deliver the option selected. It's important to remember that the "best" option is best only if the school can deliver it effectively. Principal and teachers, for example, may decide that a bilingual program is the best option for aboriginal children. Certainly there is strong research evidence to support this. If, however, there are no qualified bilingual teachers available, or if the school must compromise educational standards too greatly, then a bilingual program is no longer the best option.

Similarly, the best decision for the children in the school might be to hire an additional ESL teacher to teach a family-grouped grade one, two and three class. But what is clearly the best solution for the children is suddenly no solution at all when the school district informs the staff that there is no money in the budget for hiring an additional teacher and, even if there were, another school with six children with special needs has higher priority. Again, the best choice is an impossible one and alternatives must be found.

It's clear, then, that as we attempt to plan educational programs for ESL children, we'll face the same obstacles over and over again—someone in an administrative position who tells us, "It's a good idea and we know it's important, but there's no money." On rare occasions, an emergency fund can be tapped or outside funding sources can be found but, usually, the plan falls by the wayside.

After a while, some teachers stop asking for anything that costs money because they know in advance what the answer will be. This is a mistake. Good education is often expensive and we can be absolutely certain that no one will volunteer to give a school the money or the additional teacher or whatever else is needed if no one bothers to ask.

More central to this discussion, however, is the question—just how important is money, anyway? The quick answer is "very" but, of course, when there is none, we learn to make do. Making do in ESL classrooms has led to some very creative solutions. It has sent mainstream teachers back to university to learn about second language acquisition and teaching because they saw a need and responded to it. Making do has led teachers to use same-age and older English-speaking peers to help out with orientation to the school, homework and basic teaching. It led one large school district in Western Canada to experiment with using their designated ESL teacher not to teach children at all but to work with the other teachers in the school. She conducted regular professional development sessions throughout the school year and worked with teachers on a daily basis to plan effective strategies for teaching ESL children. While money is important, then, not having it can lead to creative solutions that may be just as effective—though it probably isn't wise to share this bit of insight with administrators!

*A Final Word*

A few years ago, while conducting a research project in Prince Rupert, British Columbia, I happened to be on hand when the school year began. I stood beside a kindergarten teacher named Allison McCormack as she greeted children arriving for their first day of school. Some of the children seemed unfazed by the experience but we could tell that others found this unfamiliar place full of strangers pretty scary.

I remember one little boy named Merko clinging to his mother's skirt for safety as he warily surveyed his surroundings. The wiry little five-year-old, brown hair sprouting uncontrollably from his head and blue-green eyes brimming with tears, couldn't have hidden his fear if he'd tried. His feeling was understandable, for who among us didn't suffer at least a twinge of anxiety, if not outright panic, the first time we left the security of home for the unknown terrors of school? In Merko's case, however, all this was compounded by the fact that he neither spoke nor understood the language that surrounded him.

I've thought about Merko many times over the years. By the end of his kindergarten year, his English was fluent and barely distinguishable from that of his native-speaker playmates. His was a success story, one that could have been told of many of the children in Allison McCormack's class and of others I've seen in many different places.

Other children's stories aren't so happy, however. For them, the road to bilingualism is much rockier. It was the stories of all the children, the successful and the not so successful, I've known and observed over the years that were on my mind as I wrote these pages. My hope is that by taking a closer look at children acquiring second languages, we can work together to smooth the path for all children. The same intent—to make schools friendlier places where every child can succeed—has shaped my career as a teacher. It's an awesome challenge, one we must pursue not only out of a sense of duty but also for the sheer joy of witnessing children succeed in the environment we help create.

My wish, then, is simply this: that, for all the children working to learn new languages in our classrooms, the minor successes become major and the major successes many. I hope this book has contributed in some small way to making this wish come true.

. . . . . . . . . . . . . .

# BIBLIOGRAPHY

Asher, J. "The Total Physical Response Approach to Language Learning." In *Modern Language Journal.* Vol. 53 (1969).

Ashworth, M. *The First Step on the Longer Path: Becoming an ESL Teacher.* Markham, Ontario: Pippin, 1992.

Brown, H. D. *Principles of Language Learning and Teaching.* 2nd Ed. Englewood Cliffs, New Jersey: Prentice-Hall, 1987.

Chamot, A. "The Learning Strategies of ESL Students." In *Learner Strategies in Language Learning."* A. Wenden & J. Rubin (Eds.). Englewood Cliffs, New Jersey: Prentice-Hall, 1987.

Chamot, A. & J.M. O'Malley. "The Cognitive Academic Language Learning Approach: A Bridge to the Mainstream." In *TESOL Quarterly.* Vol. 21, No. 2 (1987).

Chamot, A., J.M. O'Malley & L. Kupper. *Building Bridges: Content and Learning Strategies for ESL.* Books 1, 2 & 3. Boston, Massachusetts: Heinle & Heinle, 1992.

Cohen, A.D. "Studying Learner Strategies: How We Get Information." In *Learner Strategies in Language Learning."* A. Wenden & J. Rubin (Eds.). Englewood Cliffs, New Jersey: Prentice-Hall, 1987.

Collier, V. "Age and Rate of Acquisition of Second Language for Academic Purposes." In *TESOL Quarterly.* Vol. 21, No. 4 (1987).

Cummins, J. "Educational Implications of Mother Tongue Maintenance in Minority Language Groups." In *The Canadian Modern Language Review.* Vol. 34, No. 3 (1978).

Cummins, J. "Linguistic Interdependence and the Educational Development of Bilingual Children." In *Review of Educational Research*. Vol. 49 (1979).

Cummins, J. "Cognitive Academic Language Proficiency, Linguistic Interdependence, the Optimum Age Question and Some Other Matters." In *Working Papers on Bilingualism*. Vol. 19 (1979).

Cummins, J. "The Cross-Lingual Dimensions of Language Proficiency: Implications for Bilingual Education and the Optimal Age Issue." In *TESOL Quarterly*. Vol. 14, No. 25 (1980).

Cummins, J. "Wanted: A Theoretical Framework for Relating Language Proficiency to Academic Achievement among Bilingual Students." In *Language Proficiency and Academic Achievement*. C. Rivera (Ed.). Clevedon, England: Multilingual Matters, 1984.

Diller, K. *The Foreign Language Teaching Controversy*. Rowley, Massachusetts: Newbury, 1978.

Donaldson, M. *Children's Minds*. Glasgow, Scotland: Fontana/Collins, 1978.

Froese, V. (Ed.). *Whole-Language: Practice and Theory*. Scarborough, Ontario: Prentice-Hall Canada, 1990.

Krashen, S.D. *Second Language Acquisition and Second Language Learning*. Oxford, England: Pergamon Press, 1981.

Mohan, B. *Language and Content*. Reading, Massachusetts: Addison-Wesley, 1986.

Oxford, R. L. *Language Learning Strategies*. Boston, Massachusetts: Heinle & Heinle, 1990.

Piper, T. "Learning about Language Learning." In *Language Arts*. Vol. 65 (1986).

Piper, T. *Language for All Our Children*. Columbus, Ohio: Merrill, 1993.

Rigg, P. & V.G. Allen (Eds.). *When They Don't All Speak English*. Urbana, Illinois: National Council of Teachers of English, 1989.

Ruke-Dravina, V. *Mehrsprachigkeit im Vorschulalter*. Lund: Gleerup, 1967.

Staab, C. "Teachers' Practices with Regard to Oral Language." In *Alberta Journal of Educational Research*. Vol. 37, No. 1 (1991).

Swan, M. & B. Smith. *Learner English: A Teacher's Guide to Interference and Other Problems*. Cambridge, England: Cambridge University Press, 1987.

Swain, M. "Bibliography: Research on Immersion Education for the Majority Child." In *Canadian Modern Language Review*. Vol.32 (1976).

Swain, M. "Bilingual Education: Research and Its Implications." In *On TESOL 1979: The Learner in Focus*. C. Yorio, K. Perkins & J. Schachter (Eds.). Washington, D.C.: Teaching English to Speakers of Other Languages, 1979.

Swain, M. & S. Lapkin. *Evaluating Bilingual Education: A Canadian Case Study*. Clevedon, England: Multilingual Matters, 1982.

Swain, M. "French Immersion Programs across Canada: Research Findings." In *Canadian Modern Language Review*. Vol. 31, No. 2 (1974).

Tucker, G.R. & T.C. Gray. "The Pursuit of Equal Opportunity." In *Language and Society*. Vol. 2, No. 1 (1980).

Wells, G. *The Meaning Makers: Children Learning Language and Using Language to Learn*. Portsmouth, New Hampshire: Heinemann, 1986.

Wenden, A. & J. Rubin (Eds.). *Learner Strategies in Language Learning*. Englewood Cliffs, New Jersey: Prentice-Hall, 1987.

Zutell, J. "Learning Language at Home and at School." In *Discovering Language with Children*. G. S. Pinnell (Ed.). Urbana, Illinois: National Council of Teachers of English, 1980.

# MORE TITLES FROM THE PIPPIN TEACHER'S LIBRARY

*Helping Teachers Put Theory into Practice*

STORYWORLDS: LINKING MINDS AND IMAGINATIONS
THROUGH LITERATURE
Marlene Asselin, Nadine Pelland, John Shapiro

*Using literature to create rich opportunities for learning.*

WHOLE LANGUAGE: PRACTICAL IDEAS
Mayling Chow, Lee Dobson, Marietta Hurst, Joy Nucich

*Down-to-earth suggestions for both shared and independent reading
and writing, with special emphasis on evaluation strategies.*

THE WHOLE LANGUAGE JOURNEY
Sara E. Lipa, Rebecca Harlin, Rosemary Lonberger

*Making the transition to a literature-based, child-centered
approach to learning.*

WRITING PORTFOLIOS:
A BRIDGE FROM TEACHING TO ASSESSMENT
Sandra Murphy, Mary Ann Smith

*How portfolios can help students become active partners
in the writing process.*

THE FIRST STEP ON THE LONGER PATH:
BECOMING AN ESL TEACHER
Mary Ashworth

*Practical ides for helping children who are learning
English as a second language.*

SUPPORTING STRUGGLING READERS
Barbara J. Walker

*Building on struggling readers' strengths to help them broaden
their strategies for making sense of text.*

ORAL LANGUAGE FOR TODAY'S CLASSROOM
Claire Staab

*Integrating speaking and listening into the curriculum to help
children discover the power of language.*

AN EXCHANGE OF GIFTS:
A STORYTELLER'S HANDBOOK
Marion V. Ralston

*Imaginative activities to enhance language programs
by promoting classroom storytelling.*

THE WORD WALL: TEACHING VOCABULARY
THROUGH IMMERSION
Joseph Green

*Using mural dictionaries—word lists on walls—to strengthen
children's reading, speaking and writing skills.*

INFOTEXT: READING AND LEARNING
Karen M. Feathers

*Classroom-tested techniques for helping students overcome
the reading problems presented by informational texts.*

WRITING IN THE MIDDLE YEARS
Marion Crowhurst

*Suggestions for organizing a writing workshop approach
in the classroom.*